THE SEVEN FEASTS OF THE LORD

Leslie M. John

THE SEVEN FEASTS OF THE LORD

DIVINE APPOINTMENTS

LESLIE M. JOHN

THE SEVEN FEASTS OF THE LORD

Leslie M. John

Leslie M. John

THE SEVEN FEASTS OF THE LORD

DIVINE APPOINTMENTS

LESLIE M. JOHN

My mission is to proclaim the good news of our Lord Jesus Christ as revealed to me through Holy Bible and from various teachers, preachers, and commentators. This is my voluntary service to God in the name of His only begotten Son Lord Jesus Christ. I share the truth of knowledge of God with others with good intention of bringing them to the knowledge of the living God, the God of Abraham, the God of Isaac, the God of Jacob, and the Father of our Lord Jesus Christ. My mission is to proclaim the Gospel of Lord Jesus Christ and not to convert anyone forcibly to Christianity. One may accept or reject any or part of my writings/teachings. No offense is meant to any individual or any religion or any organization. Please visit http://www.lesliejohn.net/

Description:

This book brings out the truths about the Seven Feasts of the LORD also called Divine Appointments. It is imperative that every Christian should have knowledge about the Divine Appointments, detailed in Leviticus Chapter 23. The knowledge about "The Seven Feasts of the LORD", will increase the awareness in every believer as to how God programmed His Dispensations. This E-book will give knowledge to peruse the treasure hidden in the Holy Scripture.

"And the brethren immediately sent away Paul and Silas by night unto Berea: who coming there went into the synagogue of the Jews. These were more noble than those in Thessalonica, in that they received the word with all readiness of mind, and searched the scriptures daily, whether those things were so. Therefore many of them believed; also of honorable women who were Greeks, and of men, not a few" (Acts 17:10-12)

ISBN-10: 0989905845
ISBN-13:978-0-9899058-4-8

Leslie M. John

Contents

Leslie M. John

THE SEVEN FEASTS OF THE LORD

Leslie M. John

CHAPTER 1 OVERVIEW

There is no Nation that does not have yearly holidays. Every man, except for the most illiterate ones, on this earth tries to plan his commitments for the day or week or month or year. Many of man's plans and schedules may fail.

God is Almighty and is outside the time, and yet He has established times, and seasons for mankind. God planned meticulously man's creation, his redemption from sin, and eternal life for those who believe in Him; and for others who do not believe in Him He has prepared 'lake of fire', where fire never quenches, nor those who are there will cease gnashing their teeth.

God created man and they had fellowship with each other, but in due course of time, man disobeyed His command and, as a consequence, sin entered the world.

God blessed Jacob and renamed him as "Israel". There arose a king in Egypt who did not know who Joseph was. When the children of Israel grew in number and Pharaoh feared them and afflicted them with taskmasters and made them slaves unto himself, and in Egypt

"Now there arose up a new king over Egypt, which knew not Joseph. And he said unto his people, Behold, the people of the children of Israel are more and mightier than we: Come on, let us deal wisely with them; lest they multiply, and it come to pass, that, when there falleth out any war, they join also unto our enemies, and fight against us, and so get them up out of the land. Therefore they did set over them taskmasters to afflict them with their burdens. And they built for Pharaoh treasure cities, Pithom and Raamses. But the more they afflicted them, the more they multiplied and grew. And they were grieved because of the children of Israel. And the Egyptians made the children of Israel to serve with rigour: And they made their lives bitter with hard bondage, in morter, and in brick, and in all manner of service in the field: all their service, wherein they made them serve, was with rigour" (Exodus 1:8-14)

The children of Israel cried for mercy, unto the LORD, while they under the bondage of slavery under Pharaoh of Egypt, and God heard their cry. God chose one man, from among Israel to lead them out of the bondage, and that man was Moses.

Out of several nations on this earth, God chose one nation for Himself, and one people as His people, and God identified Himself as their God, and that nation was Israel.

God promised Israel a land that flowed with milk and honey and that land was Canaan. At the behest of God's command Moses and his brother stood before Pharaoh and demanded the release of the children of Israel from the bondage of slavery, in order that they may go three days journey, far away from the land of Egypt, and worship the LORD.

Pharaoh refused to let them go, and, therefore, had to see ten plagues come upon him and his people. Finally, after God inflicted the death of every first born in the

land of Egypt, Pharaoh released the children of Israel
from the bondage of slavery.

When the children of Israel were journeying out from
Egypt, Pharaoh and his army on chariots followed them
to get them back but God drowned them and killed
them in the Red Sea, while the children of Israel walked
on the dry ground in the midst of it.

The children of Israel came very close to the Promised
Land in a very short time, but they sent spies into the
land to find out whether or not they would be able to
conquer them and occupy the Promised Land, contrary
to the Promise God made to them that the land was
given to them for possession.

God allowed them to follow their unbelief and they
wandered for forty years in the wilderness before
Joshua and Caleb with the generations of the children
of Israel that were born in the wilderness during their
wandering only entered the Promised Land.

Before they entered the Promised Land God appointed
seven Holidays for the children of Israel and each one
was a feast for them. The children of Israel were
commanded to celebrate these feasts, according to
God's appointed time, when they come into the land of
Promised Land.

The children of Israel celebrated these festivals as God
said to them to do, and they will celebrate these feasts
in the thousand year reign of Lord Jesus Chirst after His
second coming. All the seven feasts had special

significance in the life of man commencing from his salvation to eternity.

While nations have many holidays and feasts, God of Israel, had appointed for them only seven holidays, wherein they had to celebrate the feasts. The seven feasts of the Lord are shadows of the realities that were to be fulfilled in future.

These seven feasts are divine appointments and God fulfilled the significance attached to the four of them precisely to the time as He planned them, and will fulfill the significance of the rest of the three feasts precisely according to His plan. The LORD did not fail in His plan nor will He fail in future.

In the Old Testament shadows and types are presented to us and prophesies were spoken as the LORD said. Some of them are fulfilled meticulously as prophesied, and some are yet to be fulfilled. The Law was fulfilled in Lord Jesus Christ.

The book of Leviticus provides us the knowledge of the ecclesiastical laws God gave to the children of Israel to observe concerning specific feasts in specific seasons, sacrifices and offerings that form a good shadow of the things to come in the New Testament period, when Christ himself would become the Lamb of God to be sacrificed and shed his precious blood for the remission of sins of mankind.

In the book of Leviticus Chapter 23 many such important instructions, which God told Moses to tell the children of Israel to observe, are found. The instructions specially relate to the feasts, and their observance that denote the things to be fulfilled in future.

The significant ones, which are fulfilled are the feast of Passover, the feast of unleavened bread, the feast of first-fruits (wave-sheaf [Resurrection]), and the Pentecost. The rest of the three festivals are feast of the Trumpets, feast of Day of Atonement, and the feast of the Tabernacles. Detailed instructions were given as to how they should celebrate their festivals, for example the first two of them are as follows:

"These are the feasts of the LORD, even holy convocations, which ye shall proclaim in their seasons. In the fourteenth day of the first month at even is the LORD'S passover. And on the fifteenth day of the same month is the feast of unleavened bread unto the LORD: seven days ye must eat unleavened bread. In the first day ye shall have an holy convocation: ye shall do no servile work therein. But ye shall offer an offering made by fire unto the LORD seven days: in the seventh day is an holy convocation: ye shall do no servile work therein". Leviticus 23:4-8

MONTHS AND SEASONS

In one of the ten plagues (Hail), that came upon Egypt as a consequence of Moses calling upon the wonders in the land of Egypt, in the name of the LORD, who demanded Pharaoh, through his servant Moses, to let the children of Israel go and worship him in the wilderness far beyond the idols in Egypt, the entire crops were destroyed. However, the crops in the land of Goshen, where the children of Israel lived, were spared.

The barley crops started growing later when Pharaoh yielded to the demand from the LORD though Moses that he will let the children of Israel go.

The hardening of the heart of Pharaoh resulted in more plagues upon the land of Egypt, one after another, until the LORD Himself went into midst of Egyptians and killed all the first born of Egyptians, and the first born of their cattle.

The LORD spared all the first born of the Israel who had upon their door posts the blood of the lamb applied as a sign of their belonging to the LORD. The blood of the lamb delivered from death of their first-born.

The ripening of the barley crops in the land of Egypt is called the season of "Abib" and it is also denoted as the month of "Nisan"

The Biblical way of counting was the day of the first moon after the crops of barley in Israel ripened, and it the month was 'Abib', and it denoted the beginning of the Jewish calendar. The first month was named "Nisan".

The LORD provided feast system symbolically and prophetically to make man understand his plan of salvation for man.

The months and the days in the month were as follows:

Nisan 30 days

Leslie M. John

Iyar 29 days

Sivan 30 days

Tammuz 29 days

Av 30 days

Elul 29 days

Tishri 30 days

Cheshvan 29 or 30 days

Kislev 30 or 29 days

Tevet 29 days

Shevat 30 days

Adar I (leap years only) 30 days

Adar (called Adar II in leap years) 29 days

[The gist on months is obtained from "American Tract Society Dictionary"]

OBSERVANCE OF FEASTS

The first day of the month of "Abib" (Nisan) was the day, which denoted the ripening stage of the barley, and the seasons and Jewish festivals were as follows:

Passover:

"In the fourteenth day of the first month at even is the LORD'S Passover" Leviticus 23:5

THE SEVEN FEASTS OF THE LORD

Iyer: This is the second month in the Jewish calendar that has 29 days

Sivan: This is the third month that has 30 days

The counting of the days of Passover feast, unleavened bread, Wave sheaf feast and Pentecost, were as follows:

14th day of Nisan was Passover. This corresponds to Thursday night and Friday Morning of present Gregorian calendar.

15th day of Nisan is Saturday and 16th day of Nisan is Sunday of present Gregorian calendar.

Jesus was crucified on the 14th day of the month 'Nisan' and He rose from the dead on the 16th day of Nisan.

Genesis 1 chapter gives us the information that evening and the morning is the day according to Biblical point of view and daylight hours of the day began at 6.00 AM as the first hour, thus the 12 P.M was the sixth hour of the day.

The birth of Jesus and His victory over Satan were prophesied many years before the actual happening.

The victory of Jesus over Satan was prophesied in Genesis 3:15

"And I will put enmity between thee and the woman, and between thy seed and her seed; it shall bruise thy head, and thou shalt bruise his heel".

Leslie M. John

Isaiah prophesied about the birth of Jesus in Isaiah 9:6-7, seven hundred years before His birth.

"For unto us a child is born, unto us a son is given: and the government shall be upon his shoulder: and his name shall be called Wonderful, Counsellor, The mighty God, The everlasting Father, The Prince of Peace. Of the increase of his government and peace there shall be no end, upon the throne of David, and upon his kingdom, to order it, and to establish it with judgment and with justice from henceforth even for ever. The zeal of the LORD of hosts will perform this".

Moses prophesied about Jesus Christ in Deuteronomy 18:15

"The LORD thy God will raise up unto thee a Prophet from the midst of thee, of thy brethren, like unto me; unto him ye shall hearken"

CHAPTER 2
THE SEVEN FEASTS OF THE LORD

There are seven feasts, also called the Divine Appointments, recorded in Leviticus Chapter 23 and they are:

(1) THE FEAST OF PASSOVER

(2) THE FEAST OF UNLEAVENED BREAD

(3) THE FEEAST OF FIRST-FRUITS

(4) THE FEAST OF PENTECOST

(5) THE FEAST OF TRUMPETS

(6) THE FEAST OF DAY OF ATONEMENT, AND

(7) THE FEAST OF TABERNACLES

The seven feasts described in Leviticus Chapter 23 are the "Divine Appointments" within the scope of the meaning of the Hebrew word "mow`ed" (Hebrew Strong's Number 04150).

These feasts, which are divine appointments are an overview of God's plan for mankind and cover the plan of salvation to eternity. The Old Testament details are shadows and types that were fulfilled in the New Testament as Substance and Anti-types. The Law was fulfilled by Lord Jesus Christ.

The first month of the Agricultural Calendar "Tishri" is the seventh month of the full year. The first month of their Religious Calendar is "Abib" (Exodus 13:4, Exodus 23:15, Exodus 34:18, and Deuteronomy 16:1). This was renamed as "Nisan" in due course of time when the

Leslie M. John

children of Israel were taken captive by Babylonians
(Nehemiah 2:1, Esther 3:7)

The first half of the year has three festivals called
"spring festivals" and a summer festival called
"Pentecost" and the second half of the year has three
festivals which are called "Fall Festivals". The Fall
Festivals are not celebrated by those who are in the
Church age. These three Fall festivals are celebrated by
Israelites and will be celebrated by Israelites in future.

CHAPTER 3
THE FEAST OF THE PASSOVER

The feast of the Passover was celebrated to remember the lamb which was set apart on the 10th day of the first month and the children of Israel killed it on the 14th day of the first month and applied its blood on the two side posts and on the upper door post of the houses. (Exodus 12:12)

When the LORD passed through the land of Egypt that night, he smote all the firstborn in the land of Egypt, both man and beast, but spared the first born of the Israelites.

In the New Testament John pointed to Jesus and said "Behold the Lamb of God, which taketh away the sin of the world" (John 1:29). Jesus made triumphal entry into Jerusalem on 10day of the first month and was crucified on the 14th day of the first month. (Matthew Chapters 21 and 27)

Passover is the remembrance of the deliverance of the children of Israel from the bondage of slavery in Egypt. Passover is celebrated for seven days in Israel. It is about remembrance of the killing of the lamb on 14th Nissan and applying its blood on the lintels and door posts of the houses of children of Israel by the children of Israel. This was to show that the children of Israel were redeemed from the slaughter of their firstborn.

God inflicted upon Pharaoh and all the Egyptians when Pharaoh refused to let the children of Israel go from out of Egypt. The demand to let the children of Israel to go from out of Egypt was made by Moses according to the commandment of the LORD. The LORD decided to kill the first born of every living creature in Egypt including that of the firstborn of Pharaoh and of even the captive in the dungeon. However, the children of Israel were saved from that plague. It is the blood of the Lamb that saved the children of Israel from that plague. The killing of the firstborn was on the midnight of the fourteenth day of the first month 'Abib' (Nisan).

The LORD commanded the children of Israel that they should tell their children as to how the LORD passed over their homes and saved them from the tenth plague. It was about remembering the sacrifice of the Passover Lamb and its blood that redeemed from the bondage of slavery under Pharaoh.

The LORD indeed rejoices to hear about Passover-narration from every child of God. Notwithstanding any writing done by anyone in the past and any details of Passover were elaborated, the LORD loves see every child of God remembers the Passover Lamb and/or tell or write about it.

Our God cannot tolerate any child of God worship other gods. The LORD said "Thou shalt have no other gods before me" (Exodus 20:3). He has neither given His glory to anyone before nor would He allow anyone to take His glory at any time.

Lord Jesus Christ instituted "Lord's Supper" after celebrating Passover Feast.

"And he took bread, and gave thanks, and broke it, and gave unto them, saying, This is my body which is given for you: this do in remembrance of me" (Luke 22:19)

THE SEVEN FEASTS OF THE LORD

In order to understand fully the words "this do in remembrance of me" (Luke 22:19) spoken by Lord Jesus Christ it is imperative that we should know what the LORD said to Moses and Aaron about Passover. The LORD spoke to Moses and Aaron and said to them to that they should convey HIS words to the children of Israel. Moses was the mediator between the LORD and the children of Israel.

PASSOVER:

The children of Israel were asked to eat the unleavened bread for seven days, after the 14th day, which obviously falls from 15th day of Nisan to 21st day of Nisan.

The lamb was killed on the 14th day, and the blood of the lamb was applied by Israelites on the door posts. The LORD went in to the midst of Egyptians and killed the all first born of Egyptians but spared the first born of Israelites. The Children of Israel were asked through Moses by the LORD to bring their first fruits of their harvest and the priest should wave the sheaf on behalf of the whole congregation

Exodus Chapter 12 commences with the LORD speaking to his beloved servant Moses, who was chosen to lead the children of Israel from out of the bondage of slavery into Canaan. Aaron, brother of Moses, was also with Moses when God spoke to Moses. The Promised Land, Canaan, was described by God Himself as the land 'flowing with milk and honey' (Exodus 3:8).

Leslie M. John

The children of Israel suffered under Pharaoh, who made them to be slaves under him and work hard, whereby their lives were made bitter. Pharaoh forced them to make bricks and to do all manner of service in the field with rigor (Exodus 1:14)

The LORD saw the misery of the children of Israel and heard their cry. He sent Moses and Aaron to make a demand that Pharaoh should let them go yonder three days journey from the land of Egypt into wilderness to worship God. Pharaoh refused to let them go on nine occasions when God brought upon the land of Egypt the plagues.

When God brought on them the tenth plague Pharaoh had indeed demanded that the children of Israel should leave Egypt as soon as possible and the Egyptians were ready to part with their possessions and wealth to any extent to see that the children of Israel leave the land of Egypt as soon as possible.

 It was after facing the tenth plague that Pharaoh released the children of Israel from the bondage of slavery. The tenth plague that the LORD brought on them killed the first-born of every Egyptian including that of Pharaoh. The tenth plague was so severe that in order to redeem the children of Israel, the LORD told them through Moses and Aaron that they have to obey Him in keeping the Passover meticulously to every detail in perfection.

The LORD said that when the children of Israel do exactly as He demanded of them their firstborn would be spared from the wrath of the LORD, as he passes over their homes.

THE SEVEN FEASTS OF THE LORD

The LORD spoke to Moses and Aaron and said that, that will be the beginning of the months and it will be the first month of the year to them. The month was known as 'Abib', which in later years was renamed as "Nissan".

The LORD said to them that the children of Israel should take a lamb on the tenth day of the said month, either from goat or sheep, which should be blameless. The LORD's instructions continue, thereafter. A lamb for every household, according to the house of their fathers was to be taken, and if the household was too small for the lamb, the man of the household may share the lamb with his neighbor, next to his house.

The number of persons from the neighbor may be counted by him to see that the portion in excess of what was required in that house can be shared by the neighbors. The lamb thus set apart was not a mere lamb but it was their special lamb, which was to be slain on the fourteenth day of the first month of the first year. The lamb that was to be thus set apart should be their lamb to become part of their family, as if a member of their family, and the children would play with it, until the fourteenth day of the month.

The LORD said that the whole assembly of the congregation of Israel should kill it in the evening of the fourteenth day of the first month of the first year. The household was required, then, to take the blood of the lamb and strike it on the two side posts and on the upper door post of the houses, where they were supposed to eat it.

They were asked to eat the Passover meal in a very specific way. They were not to violate any instructions from the LORD. Those were special and very important instructions. The flesh of the lamb thus set apart for

Leslie M. John

Passover sacrifice was to be roasted with fire, and eaten with unleavened bread in the night with bitter herbs. (The bitter herbs show their hard labor under Pharaoh and their slavery). The flesh was not be eaten raw, boiled, or soaked in water or moisture. . The head of the lamb, the liver, heart, and lungs should have been roasted and eaten.

They were to make sure that there would be no remains of the flesh of the lamb sacrificed. If by any reason there remains a portion of the lamb until next day it should be burnt with fire. The LORD was particular about their eating in haste. The LORD said to them that while they eat the flesh of the lamb they should have their loins girded, their shoes on their feet, and their staff in their hand, and their eating as to be in haste. It is the LORD's Supper and none of the instructions given to the children of Israel were allowed to be violated. (Their eating in haste shows that they were to leave the land of Egypt immediately after eating).

The LORD said unto the children of Israel that He will pass through the land of Egypt that night and smite every firstborn in the land of Egypt, both of man and beast. The LORD said He will execute judgment against the gods of Egypt because He is the LORD. Pharaoh and his gods took pleasure in the servitude of the children of Israel, whom the LORD loved so much.

The LORD had promised the Israel that He shall deliver them from out of the bondage of slavery. The LORD showed His power by humiliating their frog-gods, lice-gods, and all kinds of gods, whom they worshipped. God gave them plenty of frogs because they loved to worship frogs. This was the tenth plague that God was going to bring upon the Egyptians. In order that the children of Israel may escape this harsh judgment upon them, they were required to have the blood of the lamb on their door posts. The LORD said He shall passes over that home where he finds the blood of the lamb on the door posts and that the plague shall not be upon the household. This harsh punishment that was brought upon the Egyptians, Pharaoh, and his household, and the sparing of the children of Israel on the day of the Passover shall be a memorial for them, He said.

It was this memorial that was to be kept by the children of Israel. They were required to tell and retell their children about the grace of God that was shown to them. It was a feast for them, and their posterity was required to keep that feast.

The feast was holy and they were required to eat unleavened bread for seven days. The LORD told them that they should put away leaven even on the first day until the seventh day out of their houses in order that they may not be cut off. The first day was holy convocation.

The seventh day was holy convocation for them and they were required to take rest and no manner of work was to be done by them. They were only to eat and take rest on that day. They were to observe the feast of unleavened bread on the same day, because it was on that day that the LORD brought them out of the land of Egypt. Therefore, the observance of Passover feast became an ordinance for them for ever.

It was the fourteenth day of the month of the appointed month and year that the Passover lamb was killed and they were asked to keep the feast until the evening of twentieth day of the month. Whether a man

Leslie M. John

among them was a stranger or born in that land, he shall not have leaven in his house for seven days.

Moses told the children of Israel all that the LORD told him and Aaron. He gave them the special directions that they should take bunch of hyssop, and it should be dipped in the blood of the lamb and then strike the lintel and two side posts with the blood that is in the basin. He said to them that none of the children of Israel should go out from their homes until the LORD passes over and until the morning. The blood struck on the lintels and the door posts will serve as identification that the house belongs to one of the children of Israel, who will be spared from the wrath of the LORD.

 The children of Israel did as the LORD spoke to them through Moses and Aaron. It was an everlasting ordinance given to them that they and their sons should keep the Passover for ever. Moses told them that they shall keep the Passover even in the land that the LORD that He would give them as He had promised.

When their children inquire of them as to what this Passover meant, they were required to tell them that it was the sacrifice of the LORD's Passover, who passed over their houses in Egypt when He killed the first born of the Egyptians and delivered them from the bondage of slavery.

In the midnight of the fourteenth day of the appointed month, the LORD smote every first born in the land of Egypt from the first born of Pharaoh, who was on the throne even unto the captive in the dungeon and the firstborn of cattle. But every firstborn of the children of Israel, who had the blood of the lamb on the lintels and on the side posts of their homes, was spared.

THE SEVEN FEASTS OF THE LORD

The shaken Pharaoh was moved greatly in his heart and yielded to the demand of the LORD through Moses and Aaron. Pharaoh in his frenzy rose up in the night to see that every first born of the every Egyptian was killed. He rushed to see if his son was safe, but alas! Pharaoh's firstborn was also killed. He hurriedly called for Moses and Aaron by the night and asked them to leave Egypt as quickly as possible and asked them to go and worship their LORD, just as they demanded earlier. Pharaoh also told them that they should take their flocks and herds and be gone and requested to bless him. Egyptians were urgent upon the children of Israel that they should hastily leave Egypt fearing that they all would, otherwise, be dead.

The children of Israel took their dough before it was leavened, their kneading troughs and left the place. Before they left they borrowed the jewels, silver, gold and raiment from the Egyptians. The LORD showed favor to them that the Egyptians gladly gave all that they needed.

The children of Israel took all that they can from the Egyptians and left for Succoth from Rameses. The men of Israel were about six hundred thousand on foot besides women and children. They all went with their flocks, herds, and cattle.

The food that they had was of unleavened cakes made out of dough, which they brought forth from Egypt. The dough was not leavened. They were indeed driven out of Egypt because of the lament and cry that came upon Egypt by the slaughter of their firstborn by the LORD. They witnessed in their homes their firstborn was killed by the LORD.

Leslie M. John

As they hurriedly left Egypt they did not bring from
Egypt any other kind of food, and, therefore, they made
use of the dough to make cakes of unleavened bread.
The LORD helped them to have unleavened bread.
Their exodus was so fast and urgently forced upon them
that they could not tarry even for a little while there
after the firstborn of the Egyptians were killed by the
LORD.

It was on the same night that when the exodus of the
children of Israel took place from the land of Egypt that
the entire host of the LORD also went out from the land
of Egypt. It was the evening when their Passover lamb
was killed; and the midnight at which the LORD
executed judgment on Egyptians was very important in
the lives of the children of Israel.

It was the night when the firstborn of all the Egyptians
were slaughtered and it was to be much observed unto
the LORD by the children of Israel for delivering from
their slavery. They are, indeed, to remember their past
lives, when they served their masters in Egypt and made
bricks for them and did all manner of hard labor. It was
the night when they are, indeed, to remember how God
gave them plenty of Jewels, gold and silver of Egyptians
when they were leaving Egypt.

They were harassed many years and not paid their due
wages; and the LORD paid them when Egyptians forced
them to leave with plenty of affluence because they
could not tolerate the agony they suffered under the
Almighty God. The vengeance belongs to the LORD, and
rightly so, the Egyptians were punished by Him for
harassing the children of Israel, the people, whom God
loved very much. This Passover needs to be

remembered by the generation of the Children of Israel for ever and ever. It was an everlasting ordinance.

THE LORD'S SUPPER

There are four clear references (Matthew 26:26, Mark 14:22, Luke 22:19 and 1 Corinthians 11:24) where Lord Jesus Christ said, 'take eat; this is my body'. Likewise there are four clear references where Lord Jesus Christ said, 'my blood'.

Matthew, Mark and John, and Apostle Paul wrote that when Lord Jesus broke the bread he said 'take, eat; this is my body'. Luke, the historian, who touched the different themes of the subject did not write chronologically but included some other facts for us to ponder on. Likewise, after breaking the bread, the Lord took cup and when he had supped said, 'This cup is the new testament in my blood; this do ye, as oft as ye drink, in remembrance of me.

Each word said by Lord Jesus Christ at the time of Lord's Supper carries great significance. From Matthew 26:26 the noticeable phrases are: "As they were eating", "Jesus took bread", "and blessed it", "and brake it", "and gave it" , "to the disciples, "and said", "Take eat"; "this is my body"

"As they were eating" (Matt. 26:26) or "And as they did eat" (Mark 14:22) signifies that the Lord's Supper was instituted by Lord Jesus Christ, immediately after the Passover feast celebration.

The context where Jesus said, 'this is my body" in Gospels, appears at a place where there is description about Passover celebration. It was on the first day of the feast of unleavened bread; obviously it was on the night before his crucifixion.

This has direct reference to the lamb that was killed one day before the 14th Nissan by the children of Israel in the land of Egypt in obedience to the commandment of LORD through Moses and Aaron to escape from the tenth plague that was brought by the LORD in Egypt. The firstborn of every Egyptian, including that of Pharaoh, was killed on the night when the LORD Passed over the land.

The LORD redeemed the children of Israel, who were in bondage of slavery under Pharaoh. Every firstborn of the children of Israel and their household was spared from the wrath of the LORD, because they did as He commanded them to do. They were asked to kill the lamb, set apart for this purpose, on the fourteenth day of the first month of the first year and strike its blood on the lintels and door posts of their houses. The LORD did as He said to them and passed over their homes on seeing the blood of the lamb on the lintels and door posts of their homes. The next morning they left the Egypt and enjoyed freedom.

The children of Israel were asked to keep Passover for ever. Jesus, who came not to break the law, but to fulfill it, kept the Passover just before his crucifixion exactly as was required of him to do and in compliance to the instructions that were given in Exodus Chapter 12. It was the Passover feast day, and the disciples of Jesus asked him as to where would he have the feast of unleavened bread.

Luke's account of the Passover feast and Lord's Supper give few extra details such as a Jesus telling his disciples to follow a man bearing a pitcher of water, an unusual scene among Jews. The disciples are asked to follow him into the house where he enters.

The disciples then were supposed to ask the man of the house that the Master wants to know where the guest chamber is, where He along with the disciples would eat the Passover meal. The man of the house shows a large upper room where Jesus would eat the Passover meal. The disciples did just as the Master, Lord Jesus told them to do.

When the hour came Jesus sat down with his twelve disciples and expressed how much he desired to eat the Passover meal with his disciples before he suffers. The disciples would have got perplexed to hear that Jesus was going to suffer. It was feast time. The unleavened bread was to be eaten in remembrance of God's mighty power that delivered the children of Israel from the bondage of Slavery in Egypt. It was a time for Jesus and his disciples to remember how the firstborn of every Egyptian was killed but every first born of the children of Israel was spared.

It was then that Jesus says that one of his twelve disciples, who were sitting with him, to dine with him, would betray him. It was a time to celebrate the happy moments of the children of Israelites, whose first born were spared, by the LORD, so that they may be delivered from the bondage of slavery under Pharaoh, and when the disciples heard about the betrayal of Jesus by one of them, they were utterly perplexed and disturbed. Each one of them questioned Jesus, if he was the betrayer of Jesus.

Each one questioned him, "is it I?" Jesus said to them that he, who was dipping his hand with Jesus, shall betray him. The one, who was dipping his hand with Jesus at that time, was Judas Iscariot. Judas then asks Jesus if he was the one, who was going to betray him, and Jesus replied to him "Thou hast said".

Before that Jesus said that the Son of man would go as it was written of him, but he who betrays him would be cursed and better if he were not born.

Judas Iscariot was also known "son of perdition", which means destined to destruction. Judas Iscariot was indeed destined to destruction. He did not have good life after betraying Jesus on the same night; rather "he cast down the pieces of silver in the temple, and departed, and went and hanged himself". (Matthew 27:5).

Apostle Peter spoke of him saying "Now this man purchased a field with the reward of iniquity; and falling headlong, he burst asunder in the midst, and all his bowels gushed out". (Acts 1:18).

Jesus knew about the nefarious character of Judas Iscariot, and this is obvious when he said to Peter "...Have not I chosen you twelve, and one of you is a devil? He spake of Judas Iscariot the son of Simon: for he it was that should betray him, being one of the twelve" (John 6:70-71)

Simon Peter was curious to know as to who that disciple was, who was going to betray Jesus. When Jesus was asked about it, he said he would hand over the sop to the disciple who was going to betray him and gave the sop to Judas Iscariot, the son of Simon.

After the sop Satan entered Judas Iscariot, the son of Simon. Jesus said to Judas Iscariot to hasten doing what he had decided to do. None of his disciples, other than Judas Iscariot knew what would be the forthcoming events.

Some of his disciples thought that Judas had a bag with him, and Jesus was asking to go ahead and buy some valuables for poor. Judas, having received the sop, left immediately. (John 13:24-30).

This was the last time Judas was with Jesus as his disciple. It may be noted that Judas Iscariot participated in the Passover meal, but not in the Lord's Supper. The Lord's Supper followed the Passover meal.

From Luke's account we see that there were two cups, one of which was used during the Passover meal, and it was ceremonial cup. "And he took the cup, and gave thanks, and said, Take this, and divide it among yourselves" (Luke 22:17) Later, while instituting the Lord's Supper Jesus used another cup, which he called as, "...This cup is the new testament in my blood, which is shed for you".

"Likewise also the cup after supper, saying, This cup is the new testament in my blood, which is shed for you". (Luke 22:20)

Immediately after the Passover meal, "...Jesus took bread, and blessed it, and brake it, and gave it to the disciples, and said, Take, eat; this is my body. And he took the cup, and gave thanks, and gave it to them, saying, Drink ye all of it;

For this is my blood of the new testament, which is shed for many for the remission of sins. But I say unto you, I will not drink henceforth of this fruit of the vine, until that day when I drink it new with you in my Father's kingdom. And when they had sung an hymn, they went out into the mount of Olives". (Matthew 26:17-30)

Let us "do this in remembrance of me" until He comes as it is written...."For I have received of the Lord that which also I delivered unto you, That the Lord Jesus the same night in which he was betrayed took bread: And when he had given thanks, he brake it, and said, Take, eat: this is my body, which is broken for you: this do in remembrance of me.

After the same manner also he took the cup, when he had supped, saying, This cup is the new testament in my blood: this do ye, as oft as ye drink it, in remembrance of me. For as often as ye eat this bread, and drink this cup, ye do shew the Lord's death till he come. (1 Corinthians 11:23-26). Yes! This Lord's Table is for us to remember Lord's death until he comes, and then there is no need of it because we will be with Him for ever and ever. We will see Him face to face. The Lord's Table will be removed from our midst. In a sermon named "The Feast of the Lord" Charles H. Spurgeon said... "The other mark of time in the text is "till he come." Then this service is to end. There will be no more Lord's Suppers when Christ appears, because they will be needless.

CHAPTER 4
FIRSTBORN KILLED

10 the Plague:

(Exodus 11, 12, 13 and 14th Chapters)

This is the last plague that God brought on the Pharaoh and his people, who were vexed with nine plagues and pestilences earlier for holding Israelites in bondage to work for him, in slavery, at considerable lower wages. The children of God suffered under Pharaoh and made bricks for him, sometimes with the available raw material straw, and later by fetching straw from a distant places.

Pharaoh extracted work from them at paltry wages without realizing that paying less wages than they deserved was an abomination in the sight of God. The cry of Israelites did not go in vain, but ended in their deliverance from the bondage of slavery under Pharaoh, besides heaping up their lost wages

They lost enough wages in the past and even though the children of Israel never thought they would get back their wages, God kept accounts for them and gave them all they lost.

"Speak now in the ears of the people, and let every man borrow of his neighbour, and every woman of her neighbour, jewels of silver, and jewels of gold. And the LORD gave the people favour in the sight of the

Leslie M. John

Egyptians. Moreover the man Moses was very great in
the land of Egypt, in the sight of Pharaoh's servants, and
in the sight of the people" (Exodus 11:2-3)

The people of Israel borrowed from Egyptians jewels,
silver and jewels of gold at the instructions of Moses.
This was already a part of the provision of the covenant
God made with Abraham in Genesis 15:14 "And also
that nation, whom they shall serve, will I judge: and
afterward shall they come out with great substance"
Truly vengeance belongs to God

The enemy has taken away their possessions mercilessly
and God gave the children of Israel their due wages. In
Exodus 12:36 it is written, "And the LORD gave the
people favour in the sight of the Egyptians, so that they
lent unto them such things as they required. And they
spoiled the Egyptians"

Should we consider it as cheating or revenge here? No,
the legitimate wages of Israelites were withheld by
Pharaoh. His people ill-treated them before Moses
began showing miracles from God.   Now that Moses is
acclaimed leader of Israelites, Egyptians also recognized
that he is a great man of God and, therefore, gave them
all that they asked for.

It was God's dealing with the enemies of His children.
The cry of the children of God came before God and this
spoiling of Egyptians was the plan of God in favor of his
children. God was also showing to Egyptians through
all these wonders and plagues that He was the Holy God
of Israel, and greater than any of their frog-gods, lice
gods, or dog-fly gods, or any of their idols

THE SEVEN FEASTS OF THE LORD

The God of Abraham, Isaac and Jacob will never allow His glory to be taken by anybody. He is God and He will remain the only God for ever and ever. The last and final plague was to come upon Egypt now   Moses says,

" Thus saith the LORD, About midnight will I go out into the midst of Egypt"   Exodus 11:4

Until now God was instructing Moses either to tell Aaron to execute God's plan or Moses himself to execute God's plans to show God's wonders, but now God says He himself will go out into the midst of Egypt. The words of the LORD were so powerful that He said He will go out into the midst of Egypt to see that Pharaoh lets God's people go.

Similar were the ways of God in making a way for redeeming mankind from sin when He sent prophets first, but when His own people rejected all of them, God sent His one and only son Jesus Christ, who took upon himself the sin of mankind and He was crucified on the cross of Calvary.   He paid the price of redemption mankind from sin.

There is a responsibility bestowed upon man that if he accepts Jesus as personal savior he will have eternal life. God was going to see that every first born in the land of Egypt, except that of the children of God, would be killed so much in number that there would be cry in that land.

God said,

"But against any of the children of Israel shall not a dog move his tongue, against man or beast: that ye may

Leslie M. John

know how that the LORD doth put a difference between the Egyptians and Israel" Exodus 11:7

The LORD hardened Pharaoh's heart until then, in order that all the wonders may be multiplied, to show to the Egyptians, and the posterity of both Egyptians and the Children of Israel that He is THE almighty God, and no idol or anyone can stand against Him.

God called his name as "I AM THAT I AM" and he said, "Thus shalt thou say unto the children of Israel, I AM hath sent me unto you" Exodus 3:14

God did not make Moses a killer of the first born of Egyptians, but He took it upon himself to go into the midst of Egyptians, and kill every first born in Egypt, in order to make it a final appearance for Pharaoh.

God made it clear that all the first born, except for those of Israelites, in Egypt will die from the first born of Pharaoh up to the first born the maidservant that is at work behind the mill and also the first born of all the beasts of Egyptians. (Exodus 11:5)

Interestingly, there was a striking balance struck by God by not killing Moses, who was by law of the land of Egypt, was the first born of Pharaoh, but in essence he was genetically the first born son of Hebrew parents of Levite descendants, who were priests and there it is, the priests and the children of Israel were excluded from the killing of the first born in the land of Egypt

Another interesting fact is that Moses was, by law and as the first born of Pharaoh, he was entitled to the throne of Pharaoh, but he chose to obey God, and lead Israelites from out of the bondage of slavery.   Lucifer was the only one who dared to fight so straight battle with God by elevating himself to the level of God, and because of such pride that he showed, he was cast out from the presence of God.   Lucifer, who was an exalted Cherub but was cast down and he became Satan

God did not create Satan. God created him as the chief among the angels, who was a Cherubim but when he was cast out from the presence of God, he became Satan.   Here is another man who was a god to the people of Egyptians, but God made Moses a god to Pharaoh, and finally God showed that The Holy One of Israel, was above every god of this world, and every man in this world, and He finally overthrew Pharaoh and Satanic nature in him.   Pharaoh was thrown down from his exalted position to the lowest level of repute in Egypt   Even his servants blamed him for his actions

A noteworthy point is that even though God hardened the heart of Pharaoh, the choice of taking decisions was left to Pharaoh, who drove away the children of Israel from his presence at the end of tenth plague

• The Passover: (From Exodus Chapter 12) God set a pattern for Moses and Aaron and for Israelites as a whole nation that this will be the, "beginning of months: it shall be the first month of the year to you" Exodus 12:2 Now the days are counted from the beginning of the first month of the year and these are very important in calculating Passover. God said to Moses to "Speak ye unto all the congregation of Israel, saying, In the tenth day of this month they shall take to them every man a lamb, according to the house of their fathers, a lamb for an house" Exodus 12:3.

• It is the on the tenth day of the first month that they shall take to them every man a lamb.

• According to the house of their fathers, a lamb for a house - the calculation is so meticulous from the God of Israel   And if the household be too little for the lamb, let him and his neighbour next unto his house take it according to the number of the souls; every man according to his eating shall make your count for the lamb. Exodus 12:4.

• If the household is too small for the lamb they were required to share the lamb with the neighbor according to the number of the souls, depending on the capacity of a person to eat, in other words the man shall take as much number of people as can eat a lamb.

• The lamb thus taken should be without any blemish and it should be a male of the first year taken either from the sheep or from the goats .

• The lamb shall be kept until the fourteenth day and the whole assembly should kill it and eat in the evening.

• They are required to take the blood of the lamb and strike on the two side posts and on the upper post of the houses, where they eat the lamb.

• They are required to eat the flesh of the lamb in the same night after roasting it with fire and eat it with unleavened bread and with bitter herbs .

• Their posture while eating is described and it should as God commanded. They should eat it with their loins girded, their shoes on their feet, their staff in their hand and they should eat in haste.   It was the LORD's Passover. The way the Israelites were asked to eat the Passover reminds of the discipline in Armed Forces while they are guarding nations border in uniform. It was so important for the LORD that they were not supposed to eat without honoring the flesh and the blood of the Lamb, but they were to eat the Passover with all the reverence. There was a certain kind of posture ordered by God, and there was certain kind of attire they were ordered to be in, and there was a certain kind of order they needed to maintain when they were eating the Passover meal, and lastly the hastiness with which they were supposed to eat was emphasized.   It was not just a matter to ignore, but it was a matter that needed to be seriously thought of. n the New Testament we see that Jesus is called by John, as the 'lamb of God' .

• The LORD said He will pass through the land of Egypt that night, and will smite all the first born in the land of Egypt, both man and beast, executing judgment on all the gods of Egypt because he said, He is the LORD.

• The blood of the lamb that was struck by the Israelites will be their shield, and it shall be a token upon their houses, where they were, and when the LORD saw that blood He passed over their houses. The plague did not come upon them to destroy them, when the LORD smote the land of Egypt.

• Let us remember very clearly that it was the fourteenth day of the month that they ate the flesh of

Leslie M. John

the lamb, and applied the blood of the lamb on the side posts, and on the upper post of the house, and it was on the same night that the LORD passed in the land of Egypt killing all the first born, but passed over the houses of Israelites, when He saw the blood of the lamb.

• The blood of the lamb is shed on the fourteenth day and the LORD shall pass on the same night.

• The blood of the lamb was the savior of the Israelites.

• The Lamb was the one whose blood is shed.

• The Lamb was protected from the tenth day to the fourteenth day

• The Lamb was killed on the fourteenth day

• The "Lamb of God" was Jesus as John called in John 1st Chapter

• Jesus is the Savior the Father in heaven passes over us, when he sees the blood of the Lamb.

The LORD killed every first born in Egypt leaving behind a scene for cry in the place where the Egyptians were living, but for the Israelites, who lived in Goshen, on the North Eastern region of Egypt, they were all safe, and their first born were safe.

The Land of Goshen is described in Genesis 46:31-34

"And Joseph said unto his brethren, and unto his father's house, I will go up, and shew Pharaoh, and say unto him, My brethren, and my father's house, which were in the land of Canaan, are come unto me; And the men are shepherds, for their trade hath been to feed cattle; and they have brought their flocks, and their herds, and all that they have. And it shall come to pass, when Pharaoh shall call you, and shall say, What is your occupation? That ye shall say, Thy servants' trade hath been about cattle from our youth even until now, both we, and also our fathers: that ye may dwell in the land of Goshen; for every shepherd is an abomination unto the Egyptians" and in Genesis 47:1

"Then Joseph came and told Pharaoh, and said, My father and my brethren, and their flocks, and their herds, and all that they have, are come out of the land of Canaan; and, behold, they are in the land of Goshen"

The description of the saving grace of the Lord Jesus Christ defeating Satan on the cross should be told as clearly as possible, just as Israelites were asked to tell their children that Pharaoh would hardly let them go, but the LORD killed their first born and redeemed them from the bondage of the slavery.

(This text is taken from my old Book "Redemption of Man" Registered with Copyright office vide Certificate number Txu 1-570-036 Dated: August 15, 2007. The book is withdrawn from circulation and is on "In-active" Record. The text is edi0ted and re-registered   )

Leslie M. John

CHAPTER 5
THE FEAST OF THE UNLEAVENED BREAD

The Feast of the Unleavened Bread was celebrated from 15th day of the first month for seven days to honor the LORD for sparing their firstborn. This feast was celebrated with unleavened bread (Exodus 12:15).

Exodus 34:18 "The feast of unleavened bread shalt thou keep. Seven days thou shalt eat unleavened bread, as I commanded thee, in the time of the month Abib: for in the month Abib thou camest out from Egypt".

The LORD ordered the children of Israel to observe the feast of unleavened bread for seven days from the day after Passover that falls in the month of Abib (Nisan), which is the time when the ripening of the barley takes place in the land of Egypt.

This is the month when the children of Israel came out the land of Egypt. In order that we may be able to count the days in the feasts and the seasons of Abib in the months of Nisan, Sivan, Summer Draught (Apostasy), and Tishri, it is the first day of the month of Nisan that is important.

The essence of the seasons was to know the 14th day when the lamb was sacrificed and the LORD Passed over the homes of Israelites without harming them, but killing the entire first born of Egyptians.

In the New Testament it shows us the uncorrupted, sinless, Jesus who was without any blemish was crucified and was buried on the 15th day of the first month. In his burial his body did not decompose and was not corrupted. He was fully divine and fully human (Matthew 27:60)

Leaven is symbolic of sin and God's desire was that the children of Israel should be holy for seven days after celebrating the Passover feast; thus paying homage to the LORD, who delivered from the bondage of slavery under Pharaoh. The entire leaven from the house should have been removed because little leaven corrupts the whole lump.

In the New Testament period it is significant that while taking part in the Lord's Supper, one must examine oneself, if he has committed any sin, and repent of it. Paul speaks of keeping this feast "not with old leaven, neither of malice and wickedness, but with unleavened bread of sincerity and truth".

The bread and the cup are the emblems that show the broken body of Lord Jesus Christ and His shed blood on the cross for our redemption. Christ was our Passover Lamb crucified on the cross for our redemption from sin and, therefore, we should live a life of liberation from sin, in joy, praising God that we are redeemed from our sin.

"There is therefore now no condemnation to them which are in Christ Jesus, who walk not after the flesh, but after the Spirit" Romans 8:1.

Leslie M. John

Scripture exhorts us to examine ourselves take part worthily in order that we may not eat and drink of it for our damnation,

"But let a man examine himself, and so let him eat of that bread, and drink of that cup. For he that eateth and drinketh unworthily, eateth and drinketh damnation to himself, not discerning the Lord's body. For this cause many are weak and sickly among you, and many sleep. For if we would judge ourselves, we should not be judged" 1 Corinthians 11:28-31

Paul's main emphasis was that unrepentant sinners in the Church must be put away, after following the guidelines from Matthew Chapter 18, in order that they may not spoil the whole congregation in the Church. Sinner himself is a leaven in the Church, and such outrageous sinners, who do not repent of their sins, corrupt all members of the Church with their sinful life and false teachings.

Paul writes in Galatians 5:9 that "A little leaven leaveneth the whole lump". Leaven is symbolic of sin.

"Purge out therefore the old leaven, that ye may be a new lump, as ye are unleavened. For even Christ our passover is sacrificed for us: Therefore let us keep the feast, not with old leaven, neither with the leaven of malice and wickedness; but with the unleavened bread of sincerity and truth" 1 Corinthians 5:7-8

CHAPTER 6
THE FEAST OF THE FIRSTFRUITS

The feast of first-fruits is celebrated to honor the LORD who made the labor of the children of Israel in their fields fruitful. Their hard work was blessed by God and the land yielded its fruit.

The fruit that they reaped was because of the blessings from the LORD, who brought them out of Egypt to the Promised Land that flowed with milk and honey. The offering that they were commanded to make was not optional but it was a statute from the LORD to be obeyed meticulously by them.

The important feature of the feast of the first-fruits was that after the children of Israel have come into the Promised Land they were required to offer the first-fruits of the harvest.

The LORD commanded them that they should bring a sheaf of the first-fruits of their harvest to the priest. The priest shall wave the sheaf before the LORD on the morrow after the Sabbath, (the day of first-fruits), to be accepted on behalf of them. Sheaf is a bundle of cut stalks of grain. Hebrew Strong's Number 6016 is `omer translated as "Sheaf".

After offering sheaf-offering they were required to offer a male lamb without blemish of the first year for a burnt offering unto the LORD. The measure of the meat offering is fixed by the LORD and it was "two tenth deals of fine flour mingled with oil, an offering made by fire unto the LORD for a sweet savour: and the drink offering thereof shall be of wine, the fourth part of an hin"

Until the first-fruits are brought and offered to the LORD the children of Israel were not supposed to eat either bread, or parched corn, or green ears, and this was a statute for them throughout their generation in all their dwellings (cf. Leviticus 23:9-14)

It is not without any significance that the LORD commanded them to do offer the first-fruits, but this offering was a shadow of the thing to come in future, and that was Jesus Christ, who became first-fruits in His resurrection and ascension to heaven.

The fruit of Lord Jesus Christ's death upon the cross bearing our sins was the triumphant rising from the death. It was His victory over grave and He became the first-fruits of resurrection.

In Him we have life, and those of us, who die in Christ and rise when the Lord comes again will sing "O grave, where is they victory?" and those of us who will be caught up when the Lord comes again will sing "O death, where is thy sting?"

O death, where is thy sting? O grave, where is thy victory? (1 Corinthians 15:55)

The "feast of first-fruits" falls exactly on the "Resurrection day" of Lord Jesus Christ and it is the first day of the week.

FIRST FRUITS – RESURRECTIN OF JESUS

Jesus Christ fulfilled the laws of the Old Testament to become an offering that was acceptable.

"And he shall wave the sheaf before the LORD, to be accepted for you: on the morrow after the sabbath the priest shall wave it" (Leviticus 23:11)

There were several others who were resurrected when Jesus was resurrected but it is only Lord Jesus Christ who became the acceptable offering.

"For as Jonas was three days and three nights in the whale's belly; so shall the Son of man be three days and three nights in the heart of the earth". (Matthew 12:40)

Apostle Paul explains in 1 Corinthians 15:20-23 –

"But now is Christ risen from the dead, and become the firstfruits of them that slept. For since by man came death, by man came also the resurrection of the dead. For as in Adam all die, even so in Christ shall all be made alive. But every man in his own order: Christ the firstfruits; afterward they that are Christ's at his coming" (1 Corinthians 15:20-23)

Jesus suffered for our sake bearing our sin upon Him even unto death on the cross. He was buried and rose from the dead. He became the first-fruits of them that slept.

Jesus was not the first one to come alive after death. Jesus himself raised Lazarus and widow's son. Earlier in

Leslie M. John

the Old Testament Elijah did the miracle in 1 Kings 17:23

"And Elijah took the child, and brought him down out of the chamber into the house, and delivered him unto his mother: and Elijah said, See, thy son liveth.".

The difference between others coming to life and Jesus rising from the dead is that others were raised by either Jesus or by the power of God and later all of them died natural death.

The napkin and linen that was wrapped around the body of Lazarus was unbound at the command of Jesus, but when Jesus rose from the dead, the napkin that was bound on his head was nicely folded and kept separately from the linen.

Jesus had the power to lay down His life and take it back again on His own accord, whereas this was not so either in the case of Elijah or anyone else.

John 10:18 "No man taketh it from me, but I lay it down of myself. I have power to lay it down, and I have power to take it again. This commandment have I received of my Father".

Moses prophesied about Jesus Christ as early as in Deuteronomy 18:15 "The LORD thy God will raise up unto thee a Prophet from the midst of thee, of thy brethren, like unto me; unto him ye shall hearken"

"But I would not have you to be ignorant, brethren, concerning them which are asleep, that ye sorrow not, even as others which have no hope. For if we believe that Jesus died and rose again, even so them also which sleep in Jesus will God bring with him. For this we say unto you by the word of the Lord, that we which are alive and remain unto the coming of the Lord shall not prevent them which are asleep. For the Lord himself shall descend from heaven with a shout, with the voice of the archangel, and with the trump of God: and the dead in Christ shall rise first: Then we which are alive and remain shall be caught up together with them in the clouds, to meet the Lord in the air: and so shall we ever be with the Lord". (1 Thessalonians 4:13-17)

There were few significant happenings that took place after the resurrection of Jesus from the dead. When Mary did not find Jesus in the tomb she was worried, but Jesus appeared to her and Mary turned to him and tried to touch him, but Jesus asked her not to touch her,.

"Jesus saith unto her, Touch me not; for I am not yet ascended to my Father: but go to my brethren, and say unto them, I ascend unto my Father, and your Father; and to my God, and your God". (John 20:17)

There were two reasons why Jesus asked her not to touch him. . Firstly, it was because Jesus had not yet ascended to the Father in heaven, and secondly, because Mary had touched the dead body of Jesus when she was embalming his dead body. She was, therefore, unclean for seven days.

On Sunday Evening Jesus appeared to all the disciples except Thomas, who was not present at the place where they gathered.

Leslie M. John

John 20:19 "Then the same day at evening, being the first day of the week, when the doors were shut where the disciples were assembled for fear of the Jews, came Jesus and stood in the midst, and saith unto them, Peace be unto you".

Jesus came back only after eight days to the place where all the disciples were present including Thomas.

"And after eight days again his disciples were within, and Thomas with them: then came Jesus, the doors being shut, and stood in the midst, and said, Peace be unto you". (John 20:26)"

Jesus also appeared to several people as a proof of his resurrection.

"To whom also he shewed himself alive after his passion by many infallible proofs, being seen of them forty days, and speaking of the things pertaining to the kingdom of God" (Acts 1:3)

The final words in the book of John were very important inasmuch as Thomas his disciple doubted his resurrection.

"And Thomas answered and said unto him, My Lord and my God. Jesus saith unto him, Thomas, because thou hast seen me, thou hast believed: blessed are they that have not seen, and yet have believed. And many other signs truly did Jesus in the presence of his disciples, which are not written in this book: But these are written, that ye might believe that Jesus is the Christ, the Son of God; and that believing ye might have life through his name" (John 20:28-31).

Hebrews 9th Chapter gives us insight as to how Jesus became the high priest for us and became a perfect tabernacle, not made with hands as in Old Testament, but he by himself entered by his own blood in to the holy place.

Christ performed the office of high priest by not only offering Himself as the Lamb of God, but also by taking His own blood and sprinkling that blood of atonement in the most holy place, the heaven. This complied with the Jewish priest entering the sanctuary to minister before God.

"But Christ being come an high priest of good things to come, by a greater and more perfect tabernacle, not made with hands, that is to say, not of this building; Neither by the blood of goats and calves, but by his own blood he entered in once into the holy place, having obtained eternal redemption for us. For if the blood of bulls and of goats, and the ashes of an heifer sprinkling the unclean, sanctifieth to the purifying of the flesh: How much more shall the blood of Christ, who through the eternal Spirit offered himself without spot to God, purge your conscience from dead works to serve the living God?" (Hebrews 9:11-14)

"And he is the head of the body, the church: who is the beginning, the firstborn from the dead; that in all things he might have the preeminence". (Colossians 1:18)

Leslie M. John

"That Christ should suffer, and that he should be the first that should rise from the dead, and should shew light unto the people, and to the Gentiles" (Acts 26:23)

It is interesting that the Peter and John disciples of Lord Jesus Christ did not take it serious that there was scripture saying that He will rise again. Mary Magdalene did not recognize Lord Jesus Christ until He called her by name.

"And said unto them, Thus it is written, and thus it behoved Christ to suffer, and to rise from the dead the third day" (Luke 24:46)

The narration of the resurrection of our Lord Jesus Christ is marvelously described in John Chapter 20.

On the first day of the week Mary Magdalene went to the sepulcher and saw that stone was taken away from the sepulcher. She was surprised to see that there was no stone laid on the sepulcher.

Before Jesus was buried the chief priests and Pharisees went to Pilate and said to him that Jesus had told that He will rise again in three days, and, therefore, a command be issued that the sepulcher be secured well until the third day, in order that the disciples of Jesus may not go and steal the body and say that He rose from the dead. Pilate agreed to their suggestion and said to them to have watch and make it secure as they can.

The chief priests and Pharisees, therefore, went and made sure that the sepulcher was secured with the seal on the stone and setting a watch. (cf. Matthew 27:62-66)

From Matthew 15:47 and Matthew 27:56 it can be seen there Mary Magdalene, was not the Mary the mother of Jesus. There were several women by the name "Mary" but here the name of Mary Magdalene is mentioned. Mary Magdalene was the woman out of whom seven devils were cast out and she was healed of evil spirits and infirmities.

And certain women, which had been healed of evil spirits and infirmities, Mary called Magdalene, out of whom went seven devils, (Luke 8:2)

Mary Magdalene ran to Simon Peter, and the other disciple (John), whom Jesus loved, and said to them that "they have taken away the Lord out of the sepulcher and we not where they have laid Him".

Mary Magdalene was the first to reach the sepulcher but there were other women also with her. Other women were Mary the mother of James, and Salome. (Cf. Mark 16:1 and Matthew 28:1)

Peter and John ran to the sepulcher but John outran Peter and reached the Sepulcher. John stooped down and looked in and saw linen clothes lying but he did not go in. Peter came following came in and went into the sepulcher and saw that linen lie there. Importantly the napkin that was wrapped around the body of Lord Jesus was not along with the linen clothes but it was found wrapped together in a place by itself.

Leslie M. John

From John 11:44 it is understood that there was napkin around the face of Lazarus whom Lord Jesus resurrected. Here we see the napkin was not along with linen but it was found in a place by itself. Then John also went into the sepulcher and saw and believed they Lord Jesus Christ rose from the dead.

Surprisingly, even though they were disciple of Lord Jesus Christ they did not know that there was scripture saying that he must rise again from the dead. There were two scriptures according to which Lord Jesus Christ should rise from the dead.

"Ought not Christ to have suffered these things, and to enter into his glory?" (Luke 24:26)

"And said unto them, Thus it is written, and thus it behoved Christ to suffer, and to rise from the dead the third day" (Luke 24:46)

The feast of the first-fruits was celebrated by the Children of Israel by bringing the first fruits of their harvest to the Lord and by offering it. It was a wave offering. It was also called Sheaf offering. The sheaf consisted of stalks of barley or of wheat (Leviticus 23:10, Numbers 18:12).

In the New Testament this is fulfilled in Christ rising from the dead uncorrupted and with glorified body on the 17th day of the first month. The Resurrection of Lord Jesus Christ is recorded in Matthew Chapter 28. Christ has become the first-fruits of them that slept. (1 Corinthians 15:20)

THE SEVEN FEASTS OF THE LORD

Leslie M. John

CHAPTER 7
THE FEAST OF PENTECOST

COUNTING THE DAY

The feast of Pentecost was celebrated to mark 50th Day after the first-fruits. The feast was also called the feast of the weeks. (Leviticus 23:16).

God Himself identified the days and commanded them to follow His commandments to honor Him. It was an ordinance that they should obey when they come into the Promised Land. He identified the day when the children of Israel came out from Egypt as the fourteenth day of the month Abib. It was the day of Passover.

"In the fourteenth day of the first month at even is the LORD'S Passover". (Leviticus 23:5)

"This day came ye out in the month Abib" (Exodus 13:4)

The time for reckoning was from the day they put the sickle to the corn. It was the day of Passover celebration, which is followed immediately by the" Feast of the unleavened bread", which was to be celebrated for seven days. The first day of this seven-day festival, ("Feast of the unleavened bread"), was the "Sabbath" Day", and the next day after the "Sabbath" was the "first-fruits". Each Sabbath-week had seven days, and the next day after the Seven Sabbaths, was the fiftieth day. It was the "feast of Pentecost". That is to say the 50th day was to be counted from the "first-fruits".

"Seven weeks shalt thou number unto thee: begin to number the seven weeks from such time as thou beginnest to put the sickle to the corn". (Deuteronomy 16:9)

"And ye shall count unto you from the morrow after the sabbath, from the day that ye brought the sheaf of the wave offering; seven sabbaths shall be complete" (Leviticus 23:15)

THE OFFERINGS

The day of Pentecost was very significant day for the children of Israel because it was on this day that they offered grain offering to the LORD from their harvest.

They were commanded to offer two loaves of two tenth deals of fine flour and baked with leaven. The size of the loaf was fixed by Law and it could not be violated. This is the first-fruits unto the LORD. Notice, the bread was to baked wit leaven. It clearly showed that the Church in future would have not only the saved children of God but also false teachers in it.

"Speak unto the children of Israel, and say unto them, When ye be come into the land which I give unto you, and shall reap the harvest thereof, then ye shall bring a sheaf of the first-fruits of your harvest unto the priest: And he shall wave the sheaf before the LORD, to be accepted for you: on the morrow after the sabbath the priest shall wave it" (Leviticus 23:10-11).

Leslie M. John

And the meat offering thereof shall be two tenth deals of fine flour mingled with oil, an offering made by fire unto the LORD for a sweet savour: and the drink offering thereof shall be of wine, the fourth part of an hin. (Leviticus 23:13)

"Ye shall bring out of your habitations two wave loaves of two tenth deals: they shall be of fine flour; they shall be baken with leaven; they are the first-fruits unto the LORD". (Leviticus 23:17)

According it International Standard Bible Encyclopedia "Jewish writers are very minute in their description of the preparation of these two loaves (Josephus, Ant, III, x, 6). According to the Mishna (Menachoth, xi.4), the length of the loaf was 7 handbreadths, its width 4, its depth 7 fingers. Le 23:18 describes the additional sacrifices required on this occasion. It was a festival of good cheer, a day of joy. Free-will offerings were to be made to the Lord (De 16:10), and it was to be marked by a liberal spirit toward the Levite, the stranger, and orphans and widows (De 16:11,14). Perhaps the command against gleaning harvest-fields has a bearing on this custom (Le 23:22)".

THE SIGNIFICANCE IN THE NEW TESTAMENT

In the New Testament when the Pentecost was fully come the Holy Spirit came upon on all those waiting at Jerusalem and they were all baptized in the Holy Spirit on the 50th Day of the first month after resurrection of Jesus.

THE SEVEN FEASTS OF THE LORD

The Day of the Resurrection of Lord Jesus Christ was precisely the day of the "first-fruits". The day of Pentecost was the 50ty day of His Resurrection. This was the day when the Church came into existence and after receiving the power the disciples went and proclaimed the Gospel of Jesus Christ (Acts 1:8, Acts 2:4)

In Acts 1:4 we read that the disciples of Jesus were commanded not to depart from Jerusalem but wait for the Promise of the Father (Luke 24:49)

"And, being assembled together with [them], commanded them that they should not depart from Jerusalem, but wait for the promise of the Father, which, [saith he], ye have heard of me"

"And suddenly there came a sound from heaven as of a rushing mighty wind, and it filled all the house where they were sitting. And there appeared unto them cloven tongues like as of fire, and it sat upon each of them. (Acts 2:2-3)

After the ascension of Jesus they returned unto Jerusalem and they went up into upper room and they all continued in prayer with one accord. As we see in Acts Chapter 1:13 the disciples of Jesus, with the women, and Mary the mother of Jesus and with his brethren were in upper room and continued with one accord in prayer and supplication.

Acts 1:13 "And when they were come in, they went up into an upper room, where abode both Peter, and James, and John, and Andrew, Philip, and Thomas, Bartholomew, and Matthew, James [the son] of

Leslie M. John

Alphaeus, and Simon Zelotes, and Judas [the brother] of James."

 The narration continues to verse 15 which says that in those days Peter stood up in the midst of all of them who were one hundred and twenty in number and spoke to them.

In Acts Chapter 2 we see that the day of Pentecost had finally come and they were all with one accord in one place. The sequence of the important feasts was the "feast of Passover", the "feast of unleavened bread", and the "feast of first-fruits" and then the "feast of Pentecost", which was the 50th day of the first-fruits. Detailed description of all the feasts is listed in Leviticus Chapter 23. On the day of Passover Jesus was crucified; on the day of first-fruits Jesus rose from the dead and on the day of Pentecost the Church was born.

Jesus is called the first-fruits as we read in 1 Corinthians 15:23 "But every man in his own order: Christ the first-fruits; afterward they that are Christ's at his coming ("first-fruits" was a figurative usage of the Cf. Ro 8:23; 16:5; 1Co 15:20,23; 16:15; Jas 1:18; Re 14:4)

After Jesus rose from the dead he asked his disciples to wait at Jerusalem to receive the power. Jesus said to them they will be his witnesses after they receive the promise of the Father and that power was the Holy Spirit. The promise of the Father that is the Holy Spirit came upon all the one hundred and twenty people including the disciples of Jesus and the mother of Jesus.

THE SEVEN FEASTS OF THE LORD

It was fiftieth day after the Passover feast. It was on Pentecost when the Holy Spirit came from heaven upon all those who were in upper room where the Church came into existence. We are not asked to wait to receive the Holy Spirit, but He takes residence in every believer at the time of accepting Jesus as Savior.

There came from heaven, not from anywhere else, a sound from heaven as of a rushing mighty wind. The sound was from heaven and it was like a rushing mighty wind. It was not wind but it was like a rushing wind and when that sound came from heaven it filled the entire house where they were sitting.

Then there appeared unto them cloven tongues like of fire, not fire, but it was like fire and it sat upon each of them. There was no exclusion, but all of them had the cloven tongues like fire, not exactly fire, upon them. "Cloven" is past participle of "cleave. That means everyone in the upper room saw the split or divided tongues like that of fire that came upon and sitting upon each of them.

When they were waiting in the upper room as Jesus commanded them to do, suddenly there came a sound from heaven like that of a rushing mighty wind, and it filled the entire house where they were sitting. Then there appeared to them split tongues like as of fire, not exactly fire, and it sat upon each one of them.

The promise of the Father was that they will not be left like orphans but the Comforter that is The Holy Spirit will be with them always. When they received the Holy Spirit they began to speak with other tongues as the Spirit gave them utterance.

Leslie M. John

They spoke in other tongues as the Spirit gave them utterance. They spoke different languages. Their speaking was not the utterance from the choices that the individuals could make, but it was as the Spirit gave them the utterance.

John said: "John answered them, saying, I baptize with water: but there standeth one among you, whom ye know not". John 1:26

Mar 1:8 I indeed have baptized you with water: but he shall baptize you with the Holy Ghost.

In Acts Chapter 2 what we see is that disciples were gathered in obedience to the commandment of Jesus. The occasion was the day of the birth of the Church; that is fiftieth day after the Passover feast and it was during the feast days in Jerusalem.

The utterances were the languages of the earth which every one of them understood. It was the time of three important feasts. Firstly, it was of Passover, secondly it was of first-fruits, and thirdly it was of Pentecost. There were Jews, devout men, out of every nation under heaven in Jerusalem.

When they all in Jerusalem heard the sound of the noise that came down from heaven like that of a mighty wind they were all surprised. There was no mighty wind but they heard the sound of the mighty wind that came down from heaven.

There was multitude of people in Jerusalem. There were Parthians, and Medes, and Elamites, and the dwellers in

Mesopotamia, and in Judaea, and Cappadocia, in Pontus, and Asia, Phrygia, and Pamphylia, in Egypt, and in the parts of Libya about Cyrene, and strangers of Rome, Jews and proselytes, Cretes and Arabians.

The text in Acts 2:5-13 does not show that these all men were circumcised Proselytes. They all understood the languages that they spoke to one another and they marveled to see the signs and wonders of God. They were all amazed and some mocked saying that they were drunk, but Peter lifted up his voice and said to them that they were not drunk. Peter said that as spoken by the Prophet Joel they all spoke in languages which were understood by all of them. (Acts 2:1-20)

Many of the hearers of the word of God believed in the Lord and were baptized and the same day about three thousand souls were added, who continued steadfastly in the "apostles' doctrine and fellowship, and in breaking of bread, and in prayers"

"And they, continuing daily with one accord in the temple, and breaking bread from house to house, did eat their meat with gladness and singleness of heart, Praising God, and having favour with all the people. And the Lord added to the church daily such as should be saved". (Acts 2:46-47)

Pentecost:

Leviticus 23:15 And ye shall count unto you from the morrow after the sabbath, from the day that ye brought the sheaf of the wave offering; seven sabbaths shall be complete:

Leslie M. John

When we count the days from the first day of "Nisan" it is the fourteenth day, which is Passover, sixteenth day is the Resurrection, and it is the fiftieth day from Resurrection is the Pentecost, when the Holy Spirit came down and dwelt with us. Thus the day of Pentecost falls on the fiftieth day, which is fifth day on 'Sivan'. The days after Sabbath and then seven Sabbaths make forty nine days, and the preceding one day before the first Sabbath make fifty days in all, which is fulfilled in the New Testament.

Thus the salvation of man is complete in Lord Jesus Christ. Now, whosoever believes in him shall not perish but have eternal life.

In the current age dispensation for New Testament believer except for the sacrament of Lord's Supper and the baptism, there are no feasts designated nor are any feasts necessary.

The feasts and seasons mentioned in the Old Testament are the shadow of things to come in the New Testament period and they are for us to remember how God achieved his purpose in the present dispensation. Jesus is the express image of the Father in heaven, and as proclaimed by Jesus himself, Jesus and the Father in heaven are one.

The works done by Jesus were fully acceptable to the Father in heaven and the Father in heaven does not require any additional works to be added as the requirement for obtaining salvation. Jesus is the high priest and the mediator for us. The salvation is achieved purely by exercising faith on the works of Lord Jesus

THE SEVEN FEASTS OF THE LORD

Christ upon the cross of Calvary, by confessing to sins to God and accepting Jesus as the Lord and savior. For the salvation of a man, even these two sacraments, which indeed follow the salvation, (Baptism and Lord's supper) are not mandatory.

The Baptism is external evidence proclaimed to the people, of the faith in Jesus shown inwardly in the heart of the man, who is saved, and the Lord's supper is done to remember the death of Christ upon the cross of Calvary.

Today is the day of salvation. Please confess your sins to Jesus Christ and be blessed. Receive Salvation and eternal life. Jesus is the Way, the truth, and the life. Holy Bible says God created man, in his own image and named him as Adam and God put him in a very comfortable place called 'the garden of Eden' and gave him a wife, whom Adam named as Eve.

God gave Adam and Eve all the freedom except for eating the forbidden fruit, which Eve and Adam ate and brought sin into this world. In order to redeem mankind from their sin God sent his one and only son, Jesus Christ, who died for our sake, was buried, rose from the dead and ascended in to heaven.

Leslie M. John

CHAPTER 8
THE LONG GAP

SALVATION BY GRACE

"For I would not, brethren, that ye should be ignorant of this mystery, lest ye should be wise in your own conceits; that blindness in part is happened to Israel, until the fulness of the Gentiles be come in" Romans 11:25

Many years before Apostle Paul wrote as to how the blindness had come to Israel, God spoke to the children of Israel through Moses, His servant, that after the "feast of Pentecost", which was also called "feast of weeks", was celebrated, there will be a long gap from the last Sabbath of that week until the first day of the seventh month, the day of holy convocation, when trumpets were to be blown to commence the "fall festivals", which show the prophetical period of end days. (cf. Leviticus 23:21-25)

The long gap, after the day of the "feast of Pentecost" until the commencement day of the "feast of trumpets", was intentionally allowed by God in order that the Gentiles may into His fold.

The LORD declared to Moses, by His authority as their God, that when the children of Israel reap the harvest of their land, they shall not reap fully, to make riddance of the corners of their fields, to gather the fruit of the entire harvest, but should leave them to the poor, and to the stranger.

The LORD thus made provision for Gentiles to come in to His fold by grace through their faith. As for the gospel, the Jews are enemies for the sake of Gentiles, but as for election they are beloved of the LORD for the sake of Abraham, Isaac, and Jacob and his descendants.

Abraham came out from "Ur" of "Chaldees", which was a place of idols and idolatry, and the people of that place, did not believe in Jehovah. (Genesis 11:27-29). Paul refers to this period and subsequent periods of time, when the Gentiles were enemies to God, and thus enemies to Israel as well.

However, the Gentiles obtained mercy though the unbelief of Israel, but in times to come God will show mercy to Israel. Paul cautioned Gentiles not to take pride to consider that they have obtained their salvation as their right or because they deserved it; but it was because Israel rejected Lord Jesus Christ, as their Messiah.

Paul asks a question and he himself answers as the Lord guided him. "Hath God cast away his people? God forbid"... "God hath not cast away his people which he foreknew.

There is a time frame for the Gentiles to come into His fold, and immediately after the consummation of that period, Lord Jesus will come again. This is the time open for Jews and Gentiles to accept Lord Jesus Christ as their savior. This is the Church age, which is also called the "Grace period"

Leslie M. John

"For as ye in times past have not believed God, yet have now obtained mercy through their unbelief: Even so have these also now not believed, that through your mercy they also may obtain mercy. For God hath concluded them all in unbelief, that he might have mercy upon all" Romans 11:30-32.

CHAPTER 9
THE FEAST OF TRUMPETS

The feast of the Trumpets is the fifth feast of the seven "Feasts of the LORD" described in Leviticus Chapter 23. These feasts were to be celebrated in two different periods of Hebrew Calendar year when they come into the Promised Land. The "feast of Trumpets" is celebrated on the first day of the seventh month.

It is God's innate nature to reveal the future events to man and warn them of the consequences if they disobeyed Him. He warned Adam and Eve in the Garden of Eden that in the day they eat "of the tree of the knowledge of good and evil" they shall die. (Cf. Genesis 2:17)

Likewise God warned the oncoming flood and destruction of mankind during the days of Noah, and He warned people of Nineveh of the destruction that was to come. He gave us warnings of the last days and of the life in eternity (Cf. Matthew Chapters 24 and 25).

God did not institute these feasts just for the purpose of remembering as to how He delivered the children of Israel from the bondage of slavery in Egypt, and how he led them through wilderness into the Promised Land, but these feasts carry great significance of the events that will come to pass in future. They showed the anti-type the "Lamb of God", Lord Jesus Christ, coming into the world to save sinners, His death, burial, resurrection, His ascension, and His coming back again to set up His kingdom.

Leslie M. John

In God's calendar of events that regulate the events of mankind on this earth there are two important phases. The first one included the program of salvation of Man, and the formation of the "One New Man" with Jews and Gentiles with equal benefits. The Second phase included Lord Jesus Christ's second coming, His thousand-year-reign, judgments of nations, the final judgment at Great White Throne.

The 'feast of Trumpets' is one such warning to the children of Israel to repent and come into the kingdom of God. The children of Israel spent four hundred and thirty years as slaves to Pharaoh in Egypt. God delivered them from their bondage of slavery, and gave His calendar of events.

God counted their deliverance date as the first year; the first year of their exodus from Egypt. In the 3rd month of the first year of their exodus from Egypt, they journeyed up to Mount Sinai, where God spoke to Moses and gave the Ten Commandments to Israel. They stayed at Sinai for one year. On the first day of first month of Second year Tabernacle was set up. After completion of one month period from the day the Tabernacle was set up God revealed the contents of Leviticus to Moses. There was a 20 days period from the day the Tabernacle was set up until they resumed their journey, during which period there was numbering of God's people. They were numbered twice, once as recorded at the beginning of book Numbers and second numbering as recorded at the end of the book of Numbers. All those who came out from Egypt died in the wilderness, and only those who were numbered second time entered the Promised Land. (cf. Exodus 12:40-41, Exodus 40:17, Numbers 10:11)

It was in the first God's calendar, after God gave details to Moses, as recorded in Leviticus Chapter 23, the Passover festival was first celebrated, and then followed sequence of festivals. The "feast of Trumpets" opens up the future events that are yet to take place.

After redeeming the children of Israel from the bondage of slavery under Pharaoh the LORD said to the children of Israel through Moses, his servant, that they should celebrate seven feasts in remembrance of how God redeemed them with his "outstretched arm" from their bondage of slavery.

God, by His command set apart the first month, "Abib" , to celebrate the "Passover festival" followed by the feast of "unleavened bread", the feast of "first-fruits", and the "feast of Pentecost". During the long gap from the "feast of Pentecost" until the second phase of festivals began, it was the time of Gentiles to come into be grafted to partake their inheritance. They were not supposed to glean their farms fully but leave portions as detailed in Leviticus chapter 23:22

"And when ye reap the harvest of your land, thou shalt not make clean riddance of the corners of thy field when thou reapest, neither shalt thou gather any gleaning of thy harvest: thou shalt leave them unto the poor, and to the stranger: I am the LORD your God". (Leviticus 23:22)

The "feast of trumpets" is celebrated on the first day of seventh month, which was "Tishri". The feast of

Leslie M. John

Trumpets is known as "Rosh Hashanah" by the Jews. The fest of trumpets is followed by 'Day of atonement' and the "feast of Tabernacles"

The "Feast of the Trumpets" was not only a memorial to remember the mighty power of God but also shows the future events. The "Feast of Trumpets" calls us for repentance of the left-behind Jews and it results in their redemption which gives them the privilege of rejoicing. The blowing of trumpets sets in the future events in different periods. The Church age will not see these three feasts in future because they will be caught to be with the Lord for ever and ever.

These future events include "Rapture" of the Church, Judgment seat of Christ, "Jacob's Trouble" and the opening of the Books (Revelation 20:12) and opening of the Gates (Revelation chapter 21 and Revelation 22:14).

Failure to keep God's commandments did not go un-noticed by God; rather He chastened them with His mighty hand. He sent them into captivity for seventy years into Babylon and they could not return until the chastisement days were fulfilled. Of the seventy-year Daniel's prophecy sixty nine are fulfilled and in the seventieth year there will be "Jacob's trouble", when the left-behind Jews will call upon the Lord to save them and God will hear their cry.

During the period of Nehemiah the children of Israel realized that they failed to keep every seventh year as Sabbatical year and because of their failure God sent them into seventy year captivity into Babylon. They all gathered on the first day of the seventh month and spoke to Ezra, the scribe, to bring the book of Law of Moses, and when he had brought the book of Law of Moses, he read from it from morning to midday and they all heard with much attention.

"And all the people gathered themselves together as one man into the street that was before the water gate; and they spake unto Ezra the scribe to bring the book of the law of Moses, which the LORD had commanded to Israel. And Ezra the priest brought the law before the congregation both of men and women, and all that could hear with understanding, upon the first day of the seventh month. And he read therein before the street that was before the water gate from the morning until midday, before the men and the women, and those that could understand; and the ears of all the people were attentive unto the book of the law". (Nehemiah 8:1-3)

Later they rejoiced in the LORD and celebrated the "Feast of Tabernacles" when they found that in the book of Law there was commandment for them to celebrate the festival.

"And they found written in the law which the LORD had commanded by Moses, that the children of Israel should dwell in booths in the feast of the seventh month" (Nehemiah 8:14)

The first trumpet was made from the horn of ram that was found caught in the thicket when Abraham was about to slay his one and only son, Isaac (Cf. Genesis Ch.22). This was developed and was used by the children of Israel for calling people to gather at one place for any important occasion such as to go for war.

Leslie M. John

The trumpets were used as recorded in Numbers 10:1-10

The LORD spoke to Moses and instructed him to make two trumpets of silver from one whole piece. The metal silver indicates redemption in the Bible, while the brass indicates judgment, and gold indicates heavenly things. These trumpets were to be used to calling of the assembly, and for commencing their journey from the place, where they were stationed, to the next place until God told them to stop. He came by dark thick cloud and rested on them as canopy to protect them. He led them by pillar of fire and pillar of cloud.

"And the LORD went before them by day in a pillar of a cloud, to lead them the way; and by night in a pillar of fire, to give them light; to go by day and night: He took not away the pillar of the cloud by day, nor the pillar of fire by night, from before the people" (Exodus 13:21-22)

When the trumpet was blown then the assembly gathered at the door of the tabernacle of the congregation. If only one trumpet was used to blow, then the princes, who were the heads of thousands of Israel, gathered before Moses. If the trumpet was blown with a sound of alarm, then the camps that were on the east went ahead. If the alarm was blown second time, then the camps that were on the south side went ahead, but when congregation was to be gathered together the trumpet was to be blown in usual sound and there was to be no alarm-sound. The responsibility of blowing the trumpets was given to the priests who were sons of Aaron. It was an ordinance for ever throughout their generations.

If they went to war in their land against enemy who oppressed them, they were supposed to blow an alarm with the trumpets, and the LORD heard them and saved them from their enemies.

The children of Israel were also commanded to blow the trumpets over their burnt offerings, over their sacrifices, and of their peace offerings, in the day of their gladness, in their solemn days, in the beginnings of their moths. God said it will be a memorial before Him and the LORD proclaimed His identity as "I am the LORD your God" (cf. Numbers 10:1-10)

Sounding the trumpets in various tunes alerted the assembly, the princes, and called for God's help in times of need. Trumpets were also sounded in their solemn days. Jericho walls fell down when the trumpets were blown according as the LORD commanded.

The sounding of the trumpet has its significance in future also When it is time for Lord Jesus Christ to come again the trumpet sound is heard.

" For the Lord himself shall descend from heaven with a shout, with the voice of the archangel, and with the trump of God: and the dead in Christ shall rise first: Then we which are alive and remain shall be caught up together with them in the clouds, to meet the Lord in the air: and so shall we ever be with the Lord". (1 Thessalonians 4:16-17)

Leslie M. John

CHAPTER 10
THE FEAST OF ATONEMENT

The feast of Atonement is the "Day of Atonement".

"Also on the tenth day of this seventh month there shall be a day of atonement: it shall be an holy convocation unto you; and ye shall afflict your souls, and offer an offering made by fire unto the LORD" (Leviticus 23:27).

The "Day of Atonement" was celebrated by Israelites on the tenth day of seventh month as a memorial of the way the High Priest went into the "Holy of Holies" and sprinkled of the blood of the goat on which the lottery fell as "for the Lord" (Leviticus 16:8-9) and also as memorial of the second goat which was the "Scapegoat". The two goats collectively were the shadow of the sacrifice of Jesus on the cross and bearing the sins of the sinner.

"And Aaron shall cast lots upon the two goats; one lot for the LORD, and the other lot for the scapegoat" (Leviticus 16:8).

This is the sixth feast of the seven feasts described in Leviticus Chapter 23.

The great Day of Atonement was the shadow of the crucifixion of Lord Jesus Christ who died on behalf of us bearing our sin outside the gates of the city. Gospel writers Matthew, Mark, and John used the word "Golgotha", which means "place of skulls".

Luke used the word "Calvary" instead of "Golgotha" and Calvary means "Cranium" which again means the same as "skull". (Matthew 27:33, Mark 15:22, Luke 23:33,

John 19:17) "For he hath made him to be sin for us, who knew no sin; that we might be made the righteousness of God in him" 2 Corinthians 5:21.

"And Aaron shall cast lots upon the two goats; one lot for the LORD, and the other lot for the scapegoat" (Leviticus 16:8 - KJV)

Darby's Translation of Leviticus 16:8 says: "And Aaron shall cast lots upon the two goats: one lot for Jehovah, and the other lot for Azazel".

The word "Azazel" is not clearly understood by anyone. The most accepted meaning is the same as "Scapegoat", which bore the confessed sins and went into the wilderness and died, never to return to the camp of Israel.

The "Scapegoat" is not Satan, which some believe it to be. The "Scapegoat" is the picture of Lord Jesus Christ, who bore our sins. This is highly misunderstood doctrine in Christian Theology. Satan did not carry the sins of any one nor does anyone need to lay one's sin on Satan to take away into wilderness.

Some believe that it was Satan, who brought sin into the world and, therefore, Satan carries sin and dies in the wilderness, but this teaching is heresy. Jesus died for our sins and he bore our sins and died on the outskirts of city. Jesus is the salvation and his blood cleansed our sins.

"For he hath made him to be sin for us, who knew no sin; that we might be made the righteousness of God in him" 2 Corinthians 5:21.

The sacrifices offered in the Old Testament period covered their sins, but they were not forgiven forever.

Leslie M. John

They had to do it again the next year. In the New Testament period we are privileged that we do not need to offer such sacrifices repeatedly. Christ died for our sake once and for all; and that was enough. Our part is to believe Jesus as our Savior and repent of our sins to him. Jesus is the mediator for us and He is our High priest.

"But Christ being come an high priest of good things to come, by a greater and more perfect tabernacle, not made with hands, that is to say, not of this building; Neither by the blood of goats and calves, but by his own blood he entered in once into the holy place, having obtained eternal redemption for us" (Hebrews 9:11-12)

"So Christ was once offered to bear the sins of many; and unto them that look for him shall he appear the second time without sin unto salvation". (Hebrews 9:28)

The blood of Jesus Christ cleansed the sins of the Old Testament Saints, and also the New Testament saints. Lord Jesus became the High Priest, after the order of Melchisedec, thus setting aside the imperfect sacrificial offerings of the Old Testament. Jesus was the Savior in the past, He is the Savior now, and He will be the Savior in future. Hebrews Chapters 9, 10 and 11 detail the way Jesus became perfect sacrifice for all.

"But Christ being come an high priest of good things to come, by a greater and more perfect tabernacle, not made with hands, that is to say, not of this building; Neither by the blood of goats and calves, but by his own blood he entered in once into the holy place, having obtained eternal redemption for us"(Hebrews 9:11-12)

THE SEVEN FEASTS OF THE LORD

"So Christ was once offered to bear the sins of many; and unto them that look for him shall he appear the second time without sin unto salvation". (Hebrews 9:28)

The blood of Jesus Christ cleansed the sins of the Old Testament Saints, and also the New Testament saints. Lord Jesus became the High Priest, after the order of Melchisedec, thus setting aside the imperfect sacrificial offerings of the Old Testament. Jesus was the Savior in the past, He is the Savior now, and He will be the Savior in future. Hebrews Chapters 9,10 and 11 detail the way Jesus became perfect sacrifice for all

The first festival of the seventh month is the "Feast of Trumpets" which was celebrated on the first day of the seventh month, the second feast of the seventh month is "The feast of Day of Atonement" which was celebrated on the 10th day of seventh month, and the third feast of the seventh month is "The Feast of Tabernacles" which was celebrated on the 15th day of the seventh month..

" And the LORD spake unto Moses, saying, Speak unto the children of Israel, saying, In the seventh month, in the first day of the month, shall ye have a sabbath, a memorial of blowing of trumpets, an holy convocation. Ye shall do no servile work therein: but ye shall offer an offering made by fire unto the LORD". (Leviticus 23:23-25)

The trumpets were blown whole day proclaiming that it was a memorial day of their deliverance from Egypt. It was unique demand from God that they were to make two trumpets from silver. The metal in the two trumpets showed the consistency of perfect unison between the Old and The New Testament where the message is one and the same. The message is

Leslie M. John

Atonement, Redemption and Justification. The way it was achieved was different yet the purpose of sacrifice, repentance and redemption was the same.

Irrespective of whether it is Old Testament saint or New Testament saint the atonement (called propitiation in the New Testament) was the same and it was the blood of Jesus Christ that saved all. Lord Jesus Christ is the Central figure in the Holy Bible.

Unless sins are cleansed by the Blood of Jesus Christ there is no salvation. Old Testament saints offered sacrifices in the way they were asked to do. The Old Testament sacrifices were not perfect in nature; yet it was not the mistake of Old Testament saints. It was ordained so by God.

The atoning sacrifices in the Old Testament only covered the sins, but the sins were not forgiven forever. They had to do it again the next year. That was a shadow of the things to come in future and the blood of Jesus Christ cleansed the sins of every one. In the New Testament period we are privileged that we do not need to offer sacrifices.

Christ died for our sake once and for all; and that was enough. Our part is to believe Jesus as our Savior and repent of our sins to him. Jesus is the mediator for us and He is our High priest.

"But Christ being come an high priest of good things to come, by a greater and more perfect tabernacle, not made with hands, that is to say, not of this building; Neither by the blood of goats and calves, but by his own blood he entered in once into the holy place, having obtained eternal redemption for us"(Hebrews 9:11-12)

THE SEVEN FEASTS OF THE LORD

"So Christ was once offered to bear the sins of many; and unto them that look for him shall he appear the second time without sin unto salvation". (Hebrews 9:28)

The blood of Jesus Christ cleansed the sins of the Old Testament Saints, and also the New Testament saints. Lord Jesus became the High Priest, after the order of Melchisedec, thus setting aside the imperfect sacrificial offerings of the Old Testament. Jesus was the Savior in the past, He is the Savior now, and He will be the Savior in future. Hebrews Chapters 9,10 and 11 detail the way Jesus became perfect sacrifice for all.

Silver speaks of Redemption. In the Old Testament there number of references where silver was paid for redemption. (Leviticus 26:17, Numbers 7:13, Deuteronomy 22:29 etc.). The "Feast of Trumpets" declares the Proclamation of Christ's work.

In the New Testament we are not redeemed with Gold and silver but with the precious blood of Jesus Christ (1 Peter 1:18) and for the deliverance we received from sin we need to proclaim the Gospel of Jesus Christ in order that others may also know Him who is the Truth. (John 14:6).

The Old Testament sacrifices were shadows of the things that were fulfilled in Christ in the New Testament. Old Testament demanded perfect obedience to the Law and Christ fulfilled the Law and gave us the Grace.

We are saved by Grace through faith in Jesus. Redemption in the Old Testament did not set aside the Law and works, but Jesus gave perfect obedience to the Law and fulfilled the requirements of the Law thus freeing us from the stringent requirements of the Law.

Leslie M. John

Christ fulfilled that which Adam did not and we are unable to fulfill and given us Grace and Truth.

"For the law was given by Moses, but grace and truth came by Jesus Christ". (John 1:17)

Did you ever wonder how God arranged the movements of two and half million children of Israel when they were journeying from Egypt to Canaan in the wilderness, treading rough roads, mountains, and be triumphant in the wars against their enemies en-route and amidst dangerous animals? It was by the usage of Trumpets that the children of Israel gathered at designated places and gave obedience to their leaders.

The horn of ram that was caught in the thicket when Abraham was trying to offer Isaac as sacrifice was used as Trumpet. Later the children of Israel developed on that and used for specific purposes ordered by God. The usage of trumpets was like calling God's help. God asked Joshua to use trumpets to bring down Jericho and its walls fell down with the blowing of trumpets (Joshua 6:20)

Those who call on the Lord Jesus for forgiveness of sins will be forgiven of their sins. When they make their call through prayer God hears their prayer. When they repent of their sins and call upon Jesus he gives them everlasting life and they will not perish. (John 3:16, 1 John 1:9).

"That if thou shalt confess with thy mouth the Lord Jesus, and shalt believe in thine heart that God hath raised him from the dead, thou shalt be saved". (Romans 10:9)

THE SEVEN FEASTS OF THE LORD

We have our victory in Jesus and we are redeemed from our sins. Lord Jesus Christ became propitiation for us, and redeemed us from sins and justified us. We call for help by prayer.

"Being justified freely by his grace through the redemption that is in Christ Jesus: Whom God hath set forth to be a propitiation through faith in his blood, to declare his righteousness for the remission of sins that are past, through the forbearance of God" (Romans 3:24-25)

The "Feast of Trumpets" in the New Testament will finally be seen when the Church is "Caught up". Israel will return to their land and have Lord Jesus Christ as their king in the thousand-year-reign, which is often called "Millennium". When the children of Israel came into the land they celebrated all the seven festivals and they will celebrate those festivals in the future also.

"And the LORD shall be seen over them, and his arrow shall go forth as the lightning: and the Lord GOD shall blow the trumpet, and shall go with whirlwinds of the south". (Zechariah 9:14)

New Testament believer is member of the Church, which is the bride of Christ, will be with the Lord Jesus Christ for ever and ever.

"For the Lord himself shall descend from heaven with a shout, with the voice of the archangel, and with the trump of God: and the dead in Christ shall rise first: Then we which are alive and remain shall be caught up together with them in the clouds, to meet the Lord in the air: and so shall we ever be with the Lord. 1Thessalonians4:16, 17

Leslie M. John

CHAPTER 11
THE FEAST OF TABERNACLES

The 'feast of Tabernacles' was celebrated by the children of Israel every year according to Hebrew Calendar, commencing on the fifteenth day of the seventh month, and it was celebrated for seven days. The Jews celebrate the "Feast of Tabernacles" even today. They believe that they will rest, in future, in the city whose founder is the Maker of this world.

THE METHOD

The LORD spoke to Moses instructing him to speak the children of Israel that on the fifteenth day of the seventh month they should celebrate the" feast of tabernacles" and it shall be for seven days unto the LORD.

The first day and the eighth day shall be holy convocation, wherein they shall do no servile work. Thereafter they shall offer an offering made by fire unto the LORD.

"These are the feasts of the LORD, which ye shall proclaim to be holy convocations, to offer an offering made by fire unto the LORD, a burnt offering, and a meat offering, a sacrifice, and drink offerings, every thing upon his day" (Leviticus 23:37)

On the day of "feast of tabernacles" they should offer "the boughs of goodly trees, branches of palm trees, and the boughs of thick trees, and willows of the brook". The LORD said them to rejoice before the LORD their God.

The celebration of the" feast of the tabernacles" was a statute for their generations and during the period of seven days they should dwell in booths to remind themselves that the LORD made the children of Israel to dwell in booths, when He delivered them from the land of Egypt. (cf. 23:41-44)

This feast has great significance to the future events, when the children of Israel will rest during the thousand-year-reign of Christ on this earth, while the believers in Christ who rose from the dead incorruptible, will be with Him for ever and ever in their transformed glorified bodies (cf. 1 Corinthians 15:51-52)

"For we which have believed do enter into rest, as he said, As I have sworn in my wrath, if they shall enter into my rest: although the works were finished from the foundation of the world" (Hebrews 4:3)

THE DELIVERANCE

"Then the LORD said unto Moses, Now shalt thou see what I will do to Pharaoh: for with a strong hand shall he let them go, and with a strong hand shall he drive them out of his land" (Exodus 6:1)

The LORD delivered the children of Israel with His mighty hand from the bondage of slavery under Pharaoh, and led them through wilderness for forty years until they reached Canaan. The ten plagues that

Leslie M. John

Pharaoh and his people went through for refusing to let the children of Israel go were so unbearable and miserable that Pharaoh finally drove out the children of Israel with a strong hand. Pharaoh did not want the children of Israel any more in Egypt. But soon after Israelites started moving out Pharaoh went after them to get them back again into Egypt but he failed. Pharaoh and his armies were drowned in the Red Sea.

THE PROTECTION

The first instance of the protection the LORD granted to the children of Israel was seen when every one of the Israelites from child to the old, and every cattle passed on the dry land in the midst of the Red Sea. The LORD kept Pharaoh's army far from them by standing in between the children of Israel and Pharaoh's army.

"And the LORD went before them by day in a pillar of a cloud, to lead them the way; and by night in a pillar of fire, to give them light; to go by day and night" (Exodus 13:21)

"...The LORD looked unto the host of the Egyptians through the pillar of fire and cloud and troubled the host of the Egyptians." (Exodus 14:24)

Apostle Paul warns Corinthians in 1 Corinthians 10:1-4 that they should not be ignorant of the fact that Israelites who were redeemed by God from slavery were under the cloud, which was not an ordinary one but the very Shekinah glory of God, throughout their journey from Egypt to Canaan.

THE SEVEN FEASTS OF THE LORD

In the very early period of their journey they passed through the sea. Their passing in the midst of Red represented their baptism. They all ate of the same spiritual meat and they all drank of the same spiritual drink and that spiritual Rock that followed them was Christ. Jesus Christ was accompanied them and was the protector and provider of Israelites in the wilderness while they journeyed on foot from Egypt to Canaan for forty years.

The two sacraments, that is, the Baptism and the communion, that we do in the present age was in the form of shadow in the Old Testament which is fulfilled in Christ when he broke the bread and asked his disciples to eat of it and drink of the cup that signified his death for our sake. When we participate in the Lord's Supper we do remember the Lord's death, burial and resurrection.

The footwear of the children of Israel did not wear until they reached Canaan. Yet, on their journey they murmured several times and angered God. Finally only Joshua and Caleb and the posterity of those started their journey only reached Canaan.

The word of God says in Deuteronomy 29:5 that the children of Israel did not have any shortage either of food, or of clothing or shelter. It was indeed a great miracle that their shoe did not wear or tear on their feet when they trod the hard path in the wilderness. The path they trod was not of smooth road as we see in our days but was hard road but the one that we see in rural areas. They did not have shopping centers to do shopping nor did they steal their clothing from somebody but God provided them supernaturally their

Leslie M. John

clothing that did not wear or tear or become old on their bodies. God protected them so wonderfully -- what a privileged people they were – what a blessed nation it was! They were a chosen generation.

God protects us, and provides our needs. By grace through faith we are saved and made equal partners with Jews. There is no difference whether we are Jews or Gentiles; we are all one in Christ and we are the body of Christ and He is the head of the Church. How privileged we are that we are called "royal priesthood" and lively stones built up as spiritual house to offer spiritual sacrifices acceptable to God by Jesus Christ1 Peter 2:5,9)

"And I have led you forty years in the wilderness: your clothes are not waxen old upon you, and thy shoe is not waxen old upon thy foot". (Deuteronomy 29:5)

THE PROVISION

The LORD provided them the heavenly bread, which was called, "Manna", and protected them during day by pillar of clouds and during the night by pillar of fire. In the New Testament we see that Jesus is our bread of life. God provided the Israelites sweet water at Marah and led them by providing all that they needed. (Exodus 15:23-25). In the New Testament we see that Jesus provides living water.

The heavenly bread that the children of Israel received was called "Manna" and like coriander seed, white and tasted like wafers made of honey. God always desired

THE SEVEN FEASTS OF THE LORD

from his people that they should remember his works
for his people and how he protected them and provided
their needs. That is the reason why God said to Moses
to fill an "Omer " of Manna for their generations that
they see the bread and remember how God led their
fathers in the wilderness after delivering them from the
bondage of slavery. (Exodus 16:31-34)

We are his people delivered from the bondage of sin
when he bore our sins on the cross and washed our sins
in his blood. The Lord now desires from us that we
remember his death, burial and resurrection by
breaking the bread and eating of it and drinking from
the cup in the order that he gave to us.

"In the last day, that great day of the feast, Jesus stood
and cried, saying, If any man thirst, let him come unto
me, and drink. He that believeth on me, as the scripture
hath said, out of his belly shall flow rivers of living
water" (John 7:37-38)

Truly the Scripture has said it so in the Old Testament
in Isaiah 58:11 (Cf. Isaiah 41:17-18, Isaiah 44:3-4, Joel
3:18)

" And the LORD shall guide thee continually, and satisfy
thy soul in drought, and make fat thy bones: and thou
shalt be like a watered garden, and like a spring of
water, whose waters fail not".

It is about the outpouring of the Holy Spirit on those
who are thirsty for Him. God remembered Israelites
who were willing to come to him after hearing the
warnings. God promised them the blessings.

Leslie M. John

Without the Spirit of God man cannot be successful in anything. All things are possible with him and those who depend upon will be successful in their lives. Jesus said he will give his peace to us and not as the world gives and he has also promised before ascension that he will send the Promise of the Father (Luke 24:49).

As Jesus promised Holy Spirit came upon his disciples who were waiting for Him. Later, as Jesus told them they proclaimed the gospel of Jesus Christ, first in Jerusalem, next in Judea and Samaria and then to the uttermost part of the earth. All those whose sins are forgiven are baptized in the Holy Spirit and He indwells them instantly.

Is it applicable only to disciples who were waiting at Jerusalem? No! It is applicable to us as well. What with the commission given to the disciples of Jesus that they should preach to every nation -- is it applicable only to them -- No! It is applicable to us as well! Obstructionists do very little for the proclamation of the Gospel of Jesus Christ; instead they delve too deep only to misinterpret the solemn scriptures and say that there is no commission now!

THE LORD DWELT AMONG THEM

On their way to Canaan, the children of Israel promised to obey the commandments given by God but they failed to keep them several times. The LORD was kind to them throughout their journey by providing them the heavenly bread and water, and protecting them from sun and darkness. On their journey to Canaan they dwelt in tabernacles, also called booths. The LORD God also came and dwelt among them but in the Tabernacle that God asked them to make according to His specifications.

It is amazing to know how the Almighty God came down from his highest abode to dwell among the children of Israel and provided their needs and accepted their worship. The same God came down in incarnation in the form of man and dwelt among men, yet men did not know. After delivering the children of Israel from the bondage of slavery the LORD spoke to Moses saying:

"And the LORD spake unto Moses, saying, Speak unto the children of Israel, saying, In the seventh month, in the first day of the month, shall ye have a sabbath, a memorial of blowing of trumpets, an holy convocation. Ye shall do no servile work therein: but ye shall offer an offering made by fire unto the LORD." (Leviticus 23:23-25)

The Gospel of John speaks undeniable truths:

In the beginning was the Word, and the Word was with God, and the Word was God. (John 1:1)

" ... And the Word was made flesh, and dwelt among us, and we beheld his glory, the glory as of the only begotten of the Father, full of grace and truth "(John 1:14)

"For God so loved the world, that he gave his only begotten Son, that whosoever believeth in him should not perish, but have everlasting life." (John 3:16)

Leslie M. John

Jesus saith unto him, I am the way, the truth, and the life: no man cometh unto the Father, but by me. (John 14:6)

John was the forerunner and witness of Jesus Christ. He gave testimony of Jesus. John said he was baptizing with water but one that comes after him but preferred before him, whose shoe's latchet he did not deserve to unloose, will baptize with Holy Spirit and with fire. All those whose sins are forgiven by Jesus will be baptized with Holy Spirit and al those who did not repent will be baptized with fire, which is the lake of fire. (Matthew 3:11). John goes further and introduced Jesus as the "Lamb of God" who takes away the sin of the world. John said that Jesus was before he was. (John 1:26-30)

THE FUTURE

The children of Israel will celebrate this "feast of tabernacles" in the "Millennium". Not only the children of Israel but all the nations will celebrate this festival as the word of God says in Zechariah 14:16-21

Zachariah prophesies about the future Jerusalem which will be for the first time a place of peace. Instead of nations rising against for war the nations will come and worship the King. The thousand year rule of King Jesus will be peaceful as was never seen before in the world history.

It will be the time when Jews will celebrate the 'feast of the tabernacles' remembering their forefathers who dwelt in booths while they were on their journey from

THE SEVEN FEASTS OF THE LORD

Egypt to Canaan. God came and dwelt among them. In the millennium Jesus will be the King over united Israel. The House of Israel and the House of Judah will be united and one as was before king Solomon and even better than that inasmuch as there was none other time where such peace exited as it would exit in the millennium under the rule of Jesus Christ.

"And it shall come to pass, that every one that is left of all the nations which came against Jerusalem shall even go up from year to year to worship the King, the LORD of hosts, and to keep the feast of tabernacles"(Zechariah 14:16)

Luke was detail oriented Physician who differentiates here from the first cup and the second cup. Jesus desired to eat the Passover with his disciples before he suffered at the cross. The Lord gave the first cup to his disciples and asked them to divide among them signifying Passover festival (Luke 22:17).

He said he will not drink the fruit of the vine any more until the kingdom of the God shall come in future, and later he took bread and gave thanks and broke it saying "This is my body which is given for you: this do in remembrance of me" (Luke 22:19).

It was not the Passover festival that we are asked to remember but it is the death of Jesus who became Passover lamb for our sake that we are asked to remember. It is the custom among Jews that during the feast of Passover they sup from four cups.

The description of one cup of Passover feast is given first and Jesus said he will sup from this cup in the

Leslie M. John

Kingdom of heaven which is the Kingdom of the Son, in the thousand year reign, when he rules literally from the throne of David. By that time the scattered ten tribes from northern kingdom of Israel and southern kingdom would have been united by the Lord as prophesied.

That was the 'New Covenant' prophesied in Jeremiah, which will be fulfilled in the "kingdom of heaven". It is the second cup that Jesus gave to his disciples that represents his blood shed for us.

As the Jews refused to accept Jesus as 'Messiah' the Gentiles had the privilege to enter into His presence. We did not become partakers of the covenant to become one with the House of Israel and/or House of Judah, but we have become partakers of the New Covenant to become the members of His body.

The Church is the bride of Christ, and those who have accepted Jesus as their personal Savior constitute the bride of Christ and in this Church there is no difference between the Jew and Gentile. "For there is no difference between the Jew and the Greek: for the same Lord over all is rich unto all that call upon him. For whosoever shall call upon the name of the Lord shall be saved". (Jeremiah 31:31,Hebrews 8:8, Romans 10:12-13, 1 Corinthians 11:23-26).

We, who are born again and redeemed by the precious blood of Jesus and not with silver or gold, should remember him, who is our savior.

"Being born again, not of corruptible seed, but of incorruptible, by the word of God, which liveth and abideth for ever " (1 Peter 1:23)

The LORD told Moses to proclaim the feasts of the LORD that they may celebrate and not forget Him.

"That your generations may know that I made the children of Israel to dwell in booths, when I brought them out of the land of Egypt: I am the LORD your God". (Leviticus 23:43)

THE REMEMBRANCE

"And the LORD spake unto Moses, saying, Speak unto the children of Israel, saying, The fifteenth day of this seventh month shall be the feast of tabernacles for seven days unto the LORD". (Leviticus 23:33-34)

The LORD asked the children of Israel to celebrate the 'feast of tabernacles' to remember the LORD's compassion, his protection and his provision to the children of Israel. The LORD said to them that they should dwell in booths during the period of this festival.

This festival is celebrated that they and their children may recollect how God redeemed them from the bondage of slavery with his mighty hand and led them through the wilderness for forty years providing them food, clothing and shelter.

Not only he provided them their needs but God came and dwelt among them. The feast of tabernacles was to start on fifteenth day of seventh month and should last

Leslie M. John

for seven days. It shall be unto the LORD. On the first day of the festival it shall be an holy convocation and similarly on the eighth day of the festival it shall be an holy convocation.

The children of Israel were asked to offer an offering made by fire unto the LORD and they were not supposed to do any servile work therein. (Leviticus 23:33-42).

Now is the time of Remembrance

In the New Testament we see Jesus accepting worship as we read in Gospels. Jesus said He and the Father are one.

"And the multitudes that went before, and that followed, cried, saying, Hosanna to the Son of David: Blessed is he that cometh in the name of the Lord; Hosanna in the highest" Matthew 21:9

A New Testament believer does not need to keep Sabbath. Jesus is our mediator on whose death the veil in the temple was rent from top to bottom indicating that the New Testament believer is free from the stringent laws of the Old Testament laws. Jesus pointed that David, when hungered entered the house of God and ate the showbread which could be eaten only by the priests. Jesus is the Lord of the Sabbath. (Matthew 12:1-8)

Apostle Paul wrote in Colossians 2:16-17 that no man should judge us in meat, or in drink or in respect of an holy day or of the new moon of the Sabbath days.

THE SEVEN FEASTS OF THE LORD

There are two commandments from Jesus that a New Testament believer has to keep and they are recorded in Mark 12:30-31 – Love thy God with all your heart and with all your soul and with all your strength and the second one is to love your neighbor as yourself.

Jesus said that his death, burial and resurrection should be remembered as often as possible.

"Then Jesus said unto them, Verily, verily, I say unto you, Except ye eat the flesh of the Son of man, and drink his blood, ye have no life in you"(John 6:53)

Leslie M. John

Leslie M. John

CHAPTER 12
SHOULD WE KEEP SABBATH?

"Remember the sabbath day, to keep it holy". (Exodus 20:8)

Although 'Sabbath' does not come under the purview of the seven feasts of the LORD, it is the fourth commandment of the Ten Commandments given to the children of Israel to keep, and there is a mention about it in Leviticus Chapter 23:3

"Six days shall work be done: but the seventh day is the sabbath of rest, a holy convocation; you shall do no work on it: it is the sabbath of the LORD in all your dwellings" (Leviticus 23:3)

Therefore it is necessary to understand about "Sabbath" also along with the seven Feasts of the LORD

The fourth commandment of the Ten Commandments given to the children of Israel was in controversy for a very long time in the history of Christianity. It was a question as to whether Sabbath needs to be observed or not, and if observed whether it is to be observed on Saturday or on Sunday. There are few facts to be considered while dealing with the Sabbath Command.

To whom was the fourth command (that is to keep Sabbath) was given

Was the fourth command there in existence before it was given

What was to be done or not to be done on the day of Sabbath

What the punishment was if there is disobedience shown to the commandment.

Before we deal with the subject of Sabbath it is essential that we go back to Genesis Chapter 2 where the details about rest are mentioned. Genesis Chapter 2:2-3 read:

"And on the seventh day God ended his work which he had made; and he rested on the seventh day from all his work which he had made. And God blessed the seventh day, and sanctified it: because that in it he had rested from all his work which God created and made".

In Genesis Chapter 1:28-31 the creation account of the sixth day is narrated. On the sixth day God created man in his own image. He created male and female on the same day although details as to how He created are given in the next chapter. There are few explicit commands given by God to man; some of them are permissive and one was highly restrictive.

The permissive commands were not optional that the man can give up on them nor did the restrictive one was there for him to disobey. God gave those commands to man to surely obey. God is the creator and He has the authority to give commands. It is not for man to say why God had given such commands to man. Man and the whole creation is God's possession.

God blessed man and woman and said to them to be fruitful, multiply, and replenish the earth and subdue it. God gave authority to them to have dominion over the fish of the sea, over the fowl of the air, and over every living creature that moves on the earth. God gave them

Leslie M. John

every herb bearing seed, every tree which bears fruit that yields seed as meat for them to eat. When the sixth day came to an end the creation was fully done by God and he said everything that he had made was very good.

GOD RESTED ON THE SEVENTH DAY

From Genesis 2:4-7 it is evident that the man lived on the earth in perfect conditions. There was no rain but there went up a mist from the earth and watered the whole face of the ground that helped every plant of the field and every herb of the field to grow. "The LORD God formed man of the dust of the ground and breathed into his nostrils the breath of life and man became a living soul".

There was a perfect rest for the man to enjoy in the presence of the LORD and have fellowship with Him. The creation of heavens and the earth and all the host of them by the God ended on the sixth day and God rested. It was God's Sabbath and not man's. It was God who rested and not man.

It is not because God was tired that He rested on the seventh day but because his creation was complete. The creation was completed in six days and on the seventh day God rested. Notice the God created and His creation was complete and He rested. It was His act and He completed it and after that He rested because there was nothing to be created after sixth day. God rested from all His work which He had made and blessed the seventh day and sanctified it.

In the commands God gave to man He has not included that man should rest on the seventh day nor did he make it as an example for man to follow. God did not tell Adam or any of his posterity until the law was given during the period of Moses. There is not a single reference in Genesis that Noah, or Abraham, or Isaac, or Jacob or his children observed seventh day as rest day before the law was given.

CHOSEN GENERATION

In Abraham was a chosen generation who came from the loins of his grand son Jacob and whom God called as "my people". (Genesis 12:7, Exodus 3:7) Abraham's son was Isaac and Isaac's son was Jacob and Jacob's sons went into Egypt as a result of famine in the land of Canaan. (Genesis 37:1) The children of Israelites were under the bondage of slavery under Pharaoh for four hundred and thirty years. (Exodus 12:40) They cried and suffered under Pharaoh and the LORD heard their prayers. The LORD saw the affliction of His people who were in Egypt and knew their sorrows (Exodus 3:7). Therefore, the LORD delivered them from the bondage of slavery under Pharaoh and made a covenant with them (Exodus 12:51).

After delivering the children of Israel from the slavery under Pharaoh God led them through wilderness to Canaan. While they were on their journey God gave them Ten Commandments to follow. Along with the Ten Commandments God also gave them promises such as:

"And said, If thou wilt diligently hearken to the voice of the LORD thy God, and wilt do that which is right in his sight, and wilt give ear to his commandments, and keep all his statutes, I will put none of these diseases upon thee, which I have brought upon the Egyptians: for I am the LORD that healeth thee". (Exodus 15:26)

"Now therefore, if ye will obey my voice indeed, and keep my covenant, then ye shall be a peculiar treasure unto me above all people: for all the earth is mine" (Exodus 19:5).

That was the essence of the Old Covenant. God spoke to Moses and said to him to give instructions to the children of Israel to keep the Ten Commandments and if they obeyed His voice and kept all His commandments none of the diseases that Egyptians suffered would come on them and they will be a peculiar treasure unto God above all people. Abraham obeyed God's voice even before the Ten Commandments were given to the children of Israel God blessed Abraham (Genesis 26:5).

God did not include the Sabbath Command in the days of Abraham. This commandment was given to the children of Israel much later in the days of Moses (Exodus 20:1-17).

God said to the children of Israel through Moses that He would show mercy unto thousands of them that love Him and keep His commandments (Exodus 20:6). One such commandment, which was fourth one of the Ten Commandments, was:

"Remember the sabbath day, to keep it holy". (Exodus 20:8)

The LORD reiterated about Sabbath in Leviticus 23:1-3

"And the LORD spake unto Moses, saying, Speak unto the children of Israel, and say unto them, Concerning the feasts of the LORD, which ye shall proclaim to be holy convocations, even these are my feasts. Six days shall work be done: but the seventh day is the sabbath of rest, an holy convocation; ye shall do no work therein: it is the sabbath of the LORD in all your dwellings"

Obviously the Ten Commandments were given to the children of Israel and the fourth Command to keep Sabbath as holy was also to them. There is not one single reference which shows that the Gentiles were asked to keep the fourth commandment.

THE PUNISHMENT FOR NOT KEEPIG SABBATH

God not only gave the commandment of Sabbath to the Nation Israel but He also detailed the punishment for not keeping the Sabbath. Exodus Ch. 31:12-18 say that the LORD spoke to Moses saying to him that he should speak to the children of Israel and affirming that truly they should keep the Sabbaths that He commanded them to keep. The LORD said that it is a sign between Him and the Nation Israel throughout their generations. The demand from God that they should keep the Sabbaths was given because they were chosen generation and they are sanctified as the people of the LORD.

They were asked to keep the Sabbath as it was holy unto them and the consequence of violation of the commandment from God was that they shall not only be cut off from among His people, but shall be put to death. God said that every one of the Nation Israel who defiles the Sabbath shall surely die.

They were asked to take perfect rest on the day of Sabbath. Six days they shall work, as commanded by God, and on the seventh day they shall do no servile work therein. God made heaven and earth and on the seventh day He rested and this pattern was to be followed by every one of the children of Israel.

It was given as a perpetual commandment along with other commandments after communing with Moses on the Mount Sinai. God wrote the Ten Commandments with his finger on the two tables of stone that became the testimony.

Later, these two tables containing The Ten Commandments were kept in the Ark of the Testimony in the most Holy of Holies of the Tabernacle as a testimony for remembrance perpetually.

DID ISRAELITES KEEP SABBATH?

"Six days shall work be done, but on the seventh day there shall be to you an holy day, a sabbath of rest to the LORD: whosoever doeth work therein shall be put to death". (Exodus 35:2)

Note the severity of the punishment God detailed for not keeping the Sabbath. God said whoever violated His commandment shall be cut off from His people and shall be put to death.

Neither they nor their sons, or their daughters, or manservant, or their maidservants, or their ox, or their donkeys, or any of their cattle or the strangers who became proselytes by showing allegiance to them and their God were allowed to do any work on the seventh day. The demand from The LORD that they should keep Sabbath was given to them because He brought them out from Egypt with a mighty hand and outstretched arm (Deuteronomy 5:12-15).

God provided the children of Israel 'manna' from heaven to eat six days a week and on the seventh day they were commanded not to go out to gather the 'manna'. They were asked to gather the heavenly bread 'manna' on the sixth day for the seventh day also and nothing more.

However, some of them went out and gathered on the sixth day more than what is required for sixth day and seventh day and some went out on the seventh day to gather the food for them. He, who gathered more, did not have extra food, nor did the one who went out to gather on the seventh day found any food. This shows that the children of Israel disobeyed God and tried to do work on seventh day. (Exodus 16:25-31)

"Ye shall kindle no fire throughout your habitations upon the sabbath day" (Exodus 35:3)

A specific incident is pointed out Numbers 15:32-36 where a case of a man who violated Sabbath is mentioned. While the children of Israel were in the wilderness they found a man who violated the fourth commandment about Sabbath. The man was gathering sticks on the day of Sabbath.

It might appear to be trivial but the violation deserved punishment according to the law. They brought the man to Moses and Aaron and before the entire congregation.

Even though law was known to Moses and Aaron, they depended on God to receive a decision about the course of action to be taken and until the time God gave instruction the man was put in a ward.

The LORD said to Moses that the man should be surely put to death and the entire congregation shall stone him with stones outside the camp. In obedience to the instructions received from the LORD they took him outside the camp and stoned him unto death.

The only permitted work on the Sabbath day was that which helps in eating food (Exodus 12:16). The very essence of the law was to point the guilt of a man and condemn him unto punishment he deserved for violating the law.

The Mosaic Law provided only for the covering of sin and did not provide any solution for complete removal of sin. It was only through the blood of Lord Jesus Christ shed on the cross that a man's sin can be completely removed. Salvation is by grace through faith in Lord Jesus Christ.

No amount of good works or keeping any of the provisions of Mosaic Law could earn salvation for anybody. The sacrifices and offerings detailed in the book of Leviticus could only provide temporary remedy for the sin of man.

Every one failed to keep one commandment or the other of the Ten Commandments given by the LORD. It is, therefore, insisting on keeping any of the Ten

Commandments to earn salvation or be justified before the Law is no more can be considered right.

Lord Jesus died once and for all for our sins, and was buried and rose from the dead without seeing any corruption of His body. Sabbath was made for man and it is not vice versa. Jesus said He was the Lord of the Sabbath.

"And he said unto them, The sabbath was made for man, and not man for the Sabbath" (Mark 2:27)

"For the Son of man is Lord even of the sabbath day" (Matthew 12:8)

It is very clear in the present dispensation that it is impossible to keep Sabbath on Saturday for the simple reason that if we fail to keep Sabbath on Saturday we have to offer either sacrifice to cover our sin or get stoned unto death.

As written in Hebrews 10:26 there remains no more sacrifice for us except for the sacrifice offered once and for all by our Lord Jesus Christ by offering Himself on the cross for our sins. Surpassing our bad works with our good works is not the solution detailed in the Scripture for violating the Sabbath.

WHY DO WE WORSHIP ON SUNDAY?

Sabbath is never changed from seventh day to eighth day but then when Jesus was crucified on the cross the veil in the temple was rent into two from top to bottom signifying that in Jesus the Mosaic Law was fulfilled and we are free from that Law. It is the resurrection day, which is Sunday that we take rest on.

Leslie M. John

Man surely needs rest one day at least in a seven day period and it is good that we take rest. It is on the seventh day rest could be taken and not particularly on Saturday. Apostle Paul says:

"Let no man therefore judge you in meat, or in drink, or in respect of an holyday, or of the new moon, or of the sabbath days" (Colossians 2:16).

In addition we see in Acts 20:7 the disciples came together on the first day of the week and broke bread. In 1 Corinthians 16:2 we see that on the first day the collections were taken and they gave as God prospered them.

As we read in Acts 15th Chapter certain men came down from Judea and misled brethren that unless they are circumcised there is no salvation for them, but then Paul and Barnabas took severe exception to this demand and in the Jerusalem Peter spoke about the yoke of Mosaic Law that they were willingly taking up again on themselves in spite of redemption from it was gained through the sacrifice of Lord Jesus Christ. It is, therefore, evident that the Church does not need to observe Sabbath.

CHAPTER 13
THE FUTURE IN NUTSHELL

ANTICHRIST

Jesus warned about Antichrist in Matthew 24:4-7 and instructed his disciples to be careful about the false prophets, false teachers, and also said to them that they need to pray that their flight may not be in winter. He instructed that they would hear of wars, rumors of wars, but all those things must come to pass, but still the end would be far beyond our expected time.

Jesus told them in John 16:33 that He spoke unto them these things, so that they may have peace, because in this world they would have tribulation. These tribulations are not similar to the great tribulation, which the Jews and the left-behind will face during the Antichrist regime.

The tribulations are the ones, which every Christian will face in his/her life, when he/she is in this world. Jesus instructed all of us to be comfortable because He has overcome the world. The 'great tribulation' is different from the usual tribulations that we face in our lives. Great tribulation would be universal, and it is not limited to a local place. It will be as the world has never seen before. It would be more severe than the one that had passed by in AD 70, when many Jews were crucified upside down on the walls of Jerusalem.

Revelation 7:14 and 15 read, "...And he said to me, These are they which came out of great tribulation, and have washed their robes, and made them white in the

Leslie M. John

blood of the Lamb. Therefore are they before the throne of God, and serve him day and night in his temple...". These are those, who come out of the 'great tribulation' and are before the throne of God.

The Church will be 'caught up' when Jesus comes in clouds. From among the left-behind 144,000 from the twelve tribes of Israel will be sealed during this time; 12,000 from each tribe except from the tribes of Dan and Ephraim. The tribes of Dan and Ephraim are guilty of idolatry.

RAPTURE

One of the important prophesies that invites our attention, curiosity and hope is about the Second Coming of the Lord Jesus Christ. Although there is no word, namely, 'rapture' in the Bible, the meaning of this word as presented in 1 Thessalonians 4:17 is 'caught up'.

The Word of God teaches us that Lord Jesus Christ returns physically to establish His Kingdom literally on this earth for one thousand years. Jude 14th verse and 15th verse show us that Enoch prophesied that the Lord will return with ten thousand of His saints to execute judgment upon all.

'Rapture' is the first phase of the Second coming of our Lord Jesus Christ, and in this phase are included all believers in Christ. 'The dead in Christ shall rise first and the living saints shall be caught up together with them in the clouds to meet the Lord in the air'.

The blessed hope given to us is that we will be with the Lord for ever. The resurrection of the dead with the glorified bodies (1 Cor.15:44) will be 'in a moment, in the twinkling of an eye at the last trump: for the trumpet shall sound, and the dead shall be raised incorruptible, and we shall be changed' (1 Cor. 15:52). This happens before the commencement of Daniel's Seventieth week which is 'great tribulation'.

"For the Lord himself shall descend from heaven with a shout, with the voice of the archangel, and with the trump of God: and the dead in Christ shall rise first: Then we which are alive and remain shall be caught up together with them in the clouds, to meet the Lord in the air: and so shall we ever be with the Lord" (1 Thessalonians 4:16-17)

THE JUDGMENT SEAT OF CHRIST

For we must all appear before the judgment seat of Christ; that every one may receive the things done in his body, according to that he hath done, whether it be good or bad. (2 Corinthians 5:10)

Every believer has to account for the deeds he has done on this earth in order to receive the rewards at the 'Bema seat of Christ' He shall stand at the judgment seat of Christ also known as 'Bema Seat of Christ' not as an unbeliever to receive judgment for punishment, but for rewards he is entitled for working for the Lord.□

During the period of time when the believer is with the Lord and after the rapture, the Lord will honor his servants for the service they rendered unto Him when they were on this earth.☐@ We are not to judge our brothers because we shall all stand before the judgment seat of Christ (Rom.14:10).

The time will come when the Lord comes and He brings to the light every hidden things of darkness, and will show the counsels that have taken place in the hearts. While God does this in the presence of every believer at the judgment seat of Christ every man will praise God (1 Cor.4:5)☐

Lord Jesus Christ is our life and He will appear in the clouds in glory to receive His own unto Himself and honor them with rewards.☐ It is not the Great white Throne judgment, when those, who have not believed in Him, will be judged for their everlasting destiny in the lake of fire along with the Satan and his angels, but the judgment seat of Christ is the raised seat where He sits as the King of kings to administer justice. There shall be no condemnation for the believers, who are in Christ, and who have not walked after the flesh, but sought to walk after the Spirit. (Rom 8:1).

God was in Christ and reconciled us unto Himself, and made us, who have trusted in Him, and confessed our sins to Him, as his heirs and did not impute our trespasses unto us, but washed our sins in the precious blood of Jesus. We are His workmanship, created in Christ unto good works and we stand worthy of our calling and deserve our rewards at the 'Bema Seat of Christ'.

It is a blessed hope for believer that he will be honored for putting on Christ and for living holy life. It is at this time, when we, the believers are with the Lord, that we will be rewarded before He reveals Himself on this earth again.

STANDING ON THE MOUNT OF OLIVES

After the seventieth week of prophesy as mentioned in Daniel 9:24 is fulfilled Lord Jesus Christ, with his bride i.e. the Church, will step on the Mount of Olives. This is the Second Advent of Lord Jesus Christ on this earth. The First Advent was when Jesus was born in Bethlehem in a Manger (Luke 2:7, 12 and 16). Lord Jesus Christ with the resurrected saints will step on the Mount of Olives which is before Jerusalem on the east side. He returns to this earth with the armies of heaven as described in Revelation 19:14. It says:

"And the armies which were in heaven followed him upon white horses, clothed in fine linen, white and clean"

When the feet of Lord Jesus Christ touch the Mount of Olives it will cleave in the midst thereof toward the east and toward the west, and there shall be a very great valley; and half of the mountain shall remove toward the north and half of it toward the south".

The people who persecuted Jesus will try to flee through this valley. This valley is called "Valley of Jehoshaphat" (Joel 3:1-2).

Leslie M. John

Leslie M. John

There was neither a valley nor is now a valley by the name of "Valley of Jehoshaphat" but this is future event. The meaning of the phrase "Valley of Jehoshaphat" is "The Lord Judges". This is the throne of Lord Jesus from where he judges the nations of this earth. This judgment is not Great White Throne judgment, but it is the judgment of what is described as "Sheep and Goat Judgment" as we read in Matthew 25:33-46.

"And his feet shall stand in that day upon the mount of Olives, which is before Jerusalem on the east, and the mount of Olives shall cleave in the midst thereof toward the east and toward the west, and there shall be a very great valley; and half of the mountain shall remove toward the north, and half of it toward the south" (Zechariah 14:4)

JACOB'S TROUBLE

The time of Jacob's trouble, is the time of 'great tribulation' when Israel will mourn for the Lord, whom they crucified and this will make a way for the national repentance. God will have mercy on Israel and will restore to them their lost kingdom.

The second coming of Jesus as seen by the left- behind Jews and unbelievers is the second appearance of Lord Jesus Christ on this earth. Then the feet of Lord Jesus stand upon the Mount Olives, and thereafter He will rule for one thousand years literally from the throne of David.

119

".. I call heaven and earth to witness against you this day, that ye shall soon utterly perish from off the land whereunto ye go over Jordan to possess it; ye shall not prolong your days upon it, but shall utterly be destroyed. And the LORD shall scatter you among the nations, and ye shall be left few in number among the heathen, whither the LORD shall lead you."
Deuteronomy 4:24-27

The great tribulation will be such as was never before in the whole history of mankind upon this earth, and this is the time when the children of Israel will surely confess that the Lord Jesus is their Messiah, and God will not go back on His words of restoring them their land, and every one's name will be found in the 'book'. (Dan.12:1)

THESSALONIANS WERE MISGUIDED.

A letter was purportedly received by Thessalonians as from Apostle Paul, misguiding them that the Lord's Day had already come.

Apostle Paul clears this misapprehension in the minds of Thessalonians that such a day will not come unless there be falling away first, and the 'man of sin', who is also called, the 'son of perdition' sits in the temple of God, proclaiming himself as God, and calling for worshippers to worship him.

This 'man of sin', who is also the 'son of perdition' is not yet revealed and such revealing will be done by God, at an appropriate time, which is known to Him only. This 'man of sin', is called the Wicked, whom the Lord shall

Leslie M. John

consume 'with the spirit of his mouth, and shall destroy
with brightness of his coming' (2 Thess. 2:1-12).

The children of Israel have not received the 'Son of
God', the love of truth, and for this reason, God will
make them believe that this 'man of sin' is their savior.
But when they realize that the 'man of sin', who
promised them peace, happiness and prosperity breaks
covenant that he promised, then will the children of
Israel will call upon the living God to have mercy on
them.

The 'man of sin' opposes exalting himself above all and
sits in the temple at Jerusalem proclaiming himself as
God. The followers of Antichrist with deceivable nature
and unrighteousness would ultimately perish because
they would have refused to accept the truth and
opposed it in his time.

"And for this cause God shall send them strong
delusion, that they should believe a lie" (2
Thessalonians 2:11)

THE MILLENNIUM

God promised the children of Israel in Ezekiel 36:24
that He will take them from among the heathen gather
all of them of their countries and bring them to their
own land. As a shepherd seeks out his flock when the
sheep are scattered, so will the Lord seek out his sheep
and deliver them from out of all places, irrespective of
the conditions under which they were scattered even if
that were the cloudy and dark day.

THE SEVEN FEASTS OF THE LORD

The Lord promised that He will bring them to their own land, promised unto them, in Genesis 12:1-3, Deut. 30:3, and Isaiah 43:6, and feed them upon the mountain of Israel by the rivers in the midst of all the inhabited country.

What seems to be impossible humanly is shown as possible in Ezekiel 37:3 where it reads, "And he said unto me, Son of man, can these bones live? And I answered, O Lord GOD, thou knowest".

Christian belief rests in faith in eternal God, who has shown time and again, that nothing is impossible with Him. If dry bones can resurrect, then the Word of God, which says, his children will be caught up to the clouds where the Jesus comes in clouds should not be doubted.

The vision Ezekiel saw in 37th Chapter verses 1to 14 gives a clear picture as to how God will unite the children of Israel, once divided into two nations, the northern kingdom, also known as Ephraim and Southern kingdom known as Benjamin and Judah.

After the death of king Solomon, the northern kingdom was ruled by Jeroboam and the southern kingdom was ruled by Rehoboam.

These two kingdoms were at war with each other. The northern kingdom, although they were descendants of Jacob, were known as Israel, while the southern kingdom was known as Jews.

The Jews and Israel were at war with each other always. Assyrians captured the northern kingdom and took

Leslie M. John

them captive, while Babylonians captured the southern kingdom and took them captive. After Persians took captive and carried away, the southern kingdom under Babylonians they could never return to the southern part of Israel.

The ten tribes from the northern kingdom (House of Israel), and the two tribes from the southern kingdom were all dispersed and scattered. The tribe of Levi, who were loyal to King David, got assimilated into both the northern kingdom and the southern kingdom.

THE JUDGMENT OF THE WICKED

 And I saw a great white throne, and him that sat on it, from whose face the earth and the heaven fled away; and there was found no place for them. And I saw the dead, small and great, stand before God; and the books were opened: and another book was opened, which is the book of life: and the dead were judged out of those things which were written in the books, according to their works. (Revelation 20:11 -12)

 This is the 'Great White Throne judgment', which is the final judgment, where every one, whose name is not found in the book of life is judged and 'death and hell will be cast into the "lake of fire". This is the second death'. (Rev. 20:14)

CHAPTER 14
INVITATION TO SALVATION

JESUS SAID

"Except a man be born again, he cannot see the kingdom of God"

What does it mean to be born-again?

"Jesus answered and said unto him, Verily, verily, I say unto thee, Except a man be born again, he cannot see the kingdom of God. Nicodemus saith unto him, How can a man be born when he is old? can he enter the second time into his mother's womb, and be born? Jesus answered, Verily, verily, I say unto thee, Except a man be born of water and of the Spirit, he cannot enter into the kingdom of God". (John 3:3-5)

Jesus Christ died for our sins; he rose from the dead and ascended into heaven. He is now seated at the right hand of the Majesty and He is coming again soon.

THIS IS HOW SIN CONQURED MAN

Holy Bible says God created man in his own image. God planted a garden eastward in Eden and he put there the man whom God called Adam. The garden was indeed beautiful with every tree pleasant to sight and good for food. The LORD God made every tree to grow from the ground, the tree of life also in the midst of the garden, and the tree of knowledge of good and evil.

Leslie M. John

The LORD God put the man into the Garden of Eden to dress it and keep it. He said to the man that he may freely eat of every tree of the garden but of the tree of knowledge of good and evil he shall not eat; and in the day he eats it he shall surely die.

God saw that man was alone and the LORD God said that the man should not be alone. He decided to give a "help meet" for man. The LORD God caused a deep sleep upon Adam and while he was sleeping God took one of the ribs of the man and made a woman out of the rib and brought to him. Adam called her as "Woman" because she was taken out of Man. God said to the man to be fruitful, multiply, replenish the earth, and subdue it and have dominion over the fish of the sea, fowl of the air and every living thing that moves on the earth. (Genesis 2:8-28).

THIS IS HOW SATAN DECEIVED MAN

The serpent, who was more subtle than any other beast of the field, deceived the woman with his enticing words. The serpent spoke to her and convinced her that God did not tell the truth.

The woman yielded to the temptation of the serpent. She saw that the tree was good for food and pleasure for the eyes and thought the tree would give her intelligence. She took of its fruit and ate and also gave to her husband and he ate it.

The eyes of both of them opened and they knew that they were naked. They made aprons for themselves with fig-leaves and when they heard the voice of God, whose name is "Jehovah Elohim" they hid themselves from his presence.

Jehovah Elohim called man and asked him where he was? The man said he feared because he was naked and hid himself. God demanded an answer from the man as to who said to him that he was naked and questioned if he had he eaten fruit of the tree that he was asked not to eat from! The man blamed woman and the woman blamed the serpent.

THE CURSE FOLLOWED

The LORD God cursed the earth for man; the woman with pain in her child labor, and God cursed serpent that the serpent would crawl all the days of his life. This resulted in Adam toiling for food; woman who was in Adam and who became his wife to be a help-mate was cursed with pain in her child-bearing.

The serpent who was not crawling before became a most loathed reptile on the earth to crawl on the earth his entire life. God put enmity between the seed of the woman and of the serpent.

Adam called the woman as "Eve" because she was the mother of all living. This is how the sin entered the world. In order to reconcile man to God, Jesus relinquished his glory in heaven and came down into this world in the form of man and lived among us.

"And I will put enmity between thee and the woman,

Leslie M. John

and between thy seed and her seed; it shall bruise thy head, and thou shalt bruise his heel". (Genesis 3:15)

GOD SENT HIS SON

"For God so loved the world, that he gave his only begotten Son, that whosoever believeth in him should not perish, but have everlasting life" (John 3:16)
Jesus said: "Therefore doth my Father love me, because I lay down my life, that I might take it again". (John 10:17)

SALVATION IS FREE OF COST

According to Bible good works alone will not get us into heaven but faith in Lord Jesus Christ alone saves us. Confession by mouth and the belief that God raised Him from the dead will get us salvation free of cost. Salvation is free. No amount of good works can get a person a place in heaven. The works will follow faith in Jesus Christ and salvation. Let the Word of God speak to our hearts.

Today is the day of salvation. Please confess your sins to Jesus Christ and be blessed. Receive Salvation and eternal life. Jesus is the Way, the truth, and the life.

Holy Bible says God created man, in his own image and named him as Adam and God put him in a very comfortable place called 'the garden of Eden' and gave him a wife, whom Adam named as Eve. God gave Adam and Eve all the freedom except for eating the forbidden fruit, which Eve and Adam ate and brought sin into this world. In order to redeem mankind from their sin God sent his one and only son, Jesus Christ, who died for our sake, was buried, rose from the dead and ascended in to heaven.

Leslie M. John

THE SEVEN FEASTS OF THE LORD

Leslie M. John